PERSONNEL ISSUES AND THE CATHOLIC SCHOOL ADMINISTRATOR

edited by
J. Stephen O'Brien
and
Margaret McBrien, R.S.M.

Published by
The National Catholic Educational Association
© 1986

TABLE OF CONTENTS

Chapter IV
New Wine in New Wineskins:
Challenge to Administrators
Muriel Young, C.D.P.

Chapter V
Justice in Teacher Termination
Mary Ann Corr, S.C., Ed.D.

Chapter VI
In Justice, the Times Demand Development
Rev. Robert Yeager, Ed.D.

Chapter VII
Comprehensive Diocesan Personnel Policies
Lois King Draina, Ed.D.

FOREWORD

This book is sponsored by the Supervision, Personnel and Curriculum section of the Schools Division of the Department of Chief Administrators of Catholic Education. It is an outgrowth of discussions held at the annual SPC advisory committee meeting in January, 1984. At that time Katherine Egan, CSJ was chairwoman of the committee.

The project grew out of the knowledge that Catholic schools must continually evaluate their personnel practices to insure equitable treatment of all personnel. At a time of renewed efforts in the areas of justice and peace within the church, personnel issues can take on ever greater importance. This book should be helpful to diocesan and school administrators in their continuing efforts to proclaim the gospel through the Catholic school. The broad experiences of the authors and their important insights into personnel issues offer concrete ways to help.

Special thanks are due to Mary V. Barnes for her help in preparing the various stages of the manuscript.

Rev. J. Stephen O'Brien
Department of Chief Administrators
NCEA

CHAPTER I
POLICIES AND PRACTICES OF GOVERNANCE AND ACCOUNTABILITY
by
M. Lourdes Sheehan, R.S.M., Ed.D.

Sister Lourdes is the Executive Director of the National Association of Boards of Education at NCEA. A former teacher, principal, superintendent and provincial superior, she has spoken extensively on questions of church governance.

People are always searching for a perfect model which would settle the matter of the governance of Catholic schools. This chapter will not settle that question. The fact is there is no one set of policies, much less practices, that operates in all Catholic schools. In spite of its image as a hierarchical organization with universally enforced norms, the church's policies and practices of governance and accountability are neither uniformly defined nor universally practiced in Catholic schools.

What really happens in schools depends on personalities, policies, and politics at the local level. Given a high degree of autonomy and significant differences in governance models among the various types of schools, it follows that no single set of policies and practices is possible or desirable. Within this context, this chapter will address the topic of governance under the four typical organizational structures for Catholic schools: parish, interparish, diocesan, and private.

A parish school is defined as an institution (elementary or secondary) which is associated with only one parish from which it receives some subsidy. Those schools are designated interparish which are supported by more than one parish. Usually the subsidy flows directly from the parishes to the school. A diocesan school is one which is not identified with any one parish or group of parishes; ordinarily the subsidy goes directly from the diocese to the school. Traditionally, private schools are those which are owned, operated, and sponsored by a religious congregation which receives no parish or diocesan subsidy.

PARISH SCHOOLS

Approximately 75 percent of the Catholic elementary and secondary schools in the United States are operated as single-parish schools.[1] Ultimately, each is the responsibility of the pastor of the parish and is subject to the same church laws that govern parishes. These state that the pastor has the exclusive right to act on behalf of the parish in all juridic affairs, is responsible for the administration of all parish goods, and within the limits of the law has the ultimate authority in the parish and therefore in the parish school. The pastor must have a finance council which functions in accordance with diocesan norms and, if the bishop requires it, a pastoral council.[2] The *Code of Canon Law* does not mention education boards or commissions; however, one should presume that where they exist the collegial body must be constituted in a manner which is consistent with existing canons, diocesan legislation, and other collegial bodies.

In practice, it is the school principal who functions as the administrator of the school and the member of the parish staff who works with the school board/committee and/or other parent groups. There is obvious accountability to the parish administrator, the pastor. A good working relationship between pastor and principal, including mutual respect and trust, is key to the effective operation of the school and ultimately the parish.

When the majority of principals were appointed by the religious congregation, hiring was not the issue it is today. The question of who hires is basic to the understanding of accountability. The parish is obligated to follow diocesan policy in this and all other education matters. However, because of differing practices and the emerging role of boards it is necessary to consider hiring practices as well as roles and relationships among parish leaders.

Recognizing that the pastor has the final word and is as a matter of fact the "employer" of the principal, Father John Gilbert believes that the pastor should make it an absolute practice that no one is hired without the involvement and consent of both the board with whom the principal works and the staff.[3] There are many ways to insure this involvement. The most common is to establish a search/interview committee. Membership includes those individuals and groups whose relationship with the principal affects the running of the school.

While the pastor should be in close communication with this committee, it does not seem essential that he attend each and every

2

meeting. It would be unfortunate if he were never involved and just received the final recommendations from the committee without the benefit of prior discussion. Somewhere between no involvement and running the committee there is a middle ground which will insure agreement on the job description and on the specific needs of the parish and school.

Standard personnel practice recognizes that the person who hires is the one ultimately responsible for evaluation and continuation of the contract. Regular discussions and a commitment to keep one another informed will provide a good basis for the more formal annual evaluation carried out at least every three years. This process should involve those other groups with which the principal relates. Most dioceses have well established processes and procedures for evaluation and offer the services of the education staff to assist both the principal and pastor. In those instances where a dispute arises over contracts, both parties have the opportunity to appeal to the diocesan arbitration and conciliation process.

How the other collegial bodies in the diocese are constituted will determine to a large extent the relationship between the principal and the school board. If the board has the understanding that it is "policy-making" and has actually hired the principal, then in a very real sense the principal is the "employee" of the board. The more common practice is where the board is constituted as consultative or advisory. There the question of relationship needs clarification, but the issue of authority need not cloud the discussion. What is crucial is that the diocese state clearly its understanding of the role of collegial group, as expressed in the canons and the documents of Vatican II.

In a very real sense, the principal is accountable to the parents who have entrusted their children to the faculty and staff of the school. While this relationship cannot strictly be put under the category of governance, it is very real and demands that the principal possess a commitment to availability and communication with all parents. If good common sense is not sufficient to bring people to this conclusion, perhaps the findings of the *Effective Catholic Schools*[4] study are. One of the most significant conclusions of this research is that one of the main characteristics of an effective school is that faculty, parents, and students share a common vision and commitment to the mission of the school. There is no way in which this goal can be achieved without time and effort being spent on communications.

The individual principal may have limited contact with either the federal, state, or local education agency, but has the responsibility to know those statutes and regulations which affect non-governmental schools. The services of the Department of Education of the United States Catholic Conference are readily available to assist in governmental matters. Regular updated communications are sent to diocesan offices regarding pending federal legislation.

Most dioceses promulgate education policies which affect parish schools directly. Technically there is a distinction between legislative statements which have the force of policy and those guidelines designated as administrative. In practice they are implemented at the parish level with the same commitment.

Depending on the size and organizational structure of the diocese, the superintendent of schools reports directly to the bishop or functions as part of an office of education and is directly accountable to the secretary or vicar for education. The impact that the diocesan arrangement has on the parish school is usually not significant. The principal needs to know such practical matters as where the responsibility for religious education rests both at the diocesan level and in the parish. Given that the principal is the administrator of the total school program, it seems advisable for that person to have the responsibility for the religious education as well. This allocation of responsibility does not in any way minimize the need for the principal and the parish director of religious education to work together as members of the parish staff for the good of all. This same principle applies at the diocesan level where the superintendent of schools should have the administrative control of the entire curriculum in the diocese. As the chief catechist the bishop has final authority for the religious education in his diocese; the clarification of accountability in this matter is especially helpful to insure the effective functioning of the school.

PRIVATE SCHOOLS

Constituting 38.5 percent of Catholic secondary schools, schools operated by religious congregations are the largest percentage of Catholic secondary schools. At the elementary level, private schools are the smallest group at 5 percent.[5] Traditionally, private schools have enjoyed the clearest lines of authority and accountability. The major superior and council of the religious community have the authority for the administration of the congregation and its works. They ordinarily appoint the principal of the school who is also a member of the congregation and in practice enjoys almost total autonomy in the daily administration of the institution.

The authority of the bishop in the areas of religious education and the Catholicity of the school is recognized, but for all practical purposes never exercised. Relations with the diocesan school office are usually cordial but distant, probably because there is no involvement in either finances or personnel. While the lines of authority remain clear as far as ownership and sponsorship of private Catholic schools are concerned, there seems to be a changing climate regarding the schools' operations.

As more religious congregations establish boards with non-congregational members, the issues of governance and management need clarification. More often than not, the key point of discussion is the hiring of the principal and therefore the relation of that person to the religious congregation and to the board. When the administrator is a member of the congregation that issue is not as complicated as it is when a lay person assumes that position. There are many models which seem to be working; what is essential is that there be a clear understanding between the congregational leadership and the board of directors of the school.

Finances are always an area of concern. Most statements of relations with boards of directors give the responsibility for the operations of the school to the local board with the understanding that the operating budget will be a balanced one. An unresolved issue for most congregations and their schools is the question of responsibility for capital improvements and repairs. One approach may be for the congregation to recognize its role as "landlord" and function in this way in regard to major repairs and renovations. This model assumes that the board of directors will function as a "tenant" and may allocate a percentage of the operating budget as either rent or contingency for upkeep.

The person who most needs clarity in the question of roles and relationships is the principal. It does not seem wise to rely on either membership or chance to insure that the school will be administered in accordance with clear policies and guidelines. The question of the principal's accountability in the private school is different in those instances where there is another person designated as the president of the school. Where both of the individuals are members of the same congregation, they probably enjoy the same understanding as to the traditional role definitions in this arrangement. Where a member of the congregation serves as president and a lay person functions as principal, much time and energy should be given to clarifying responsibilities. Perhaps there are some analogies between this model and the functioning relationship between the pastor and principal at the parish school.

DIOCESAN SCHOOLS

Diocesan schools comprise 35.5 percent of the secondary and 4.2 percent of the elementary Catholic schools in this country.[6] Organizationally, the diocesan school is directly accountable to the diocese; practically, this usually means that the responsibility is to the bishop through the superintendent of schools and some type of board structure. Since the practice of designating elementary schools as diocesan seems to be relatively new, there is no traditional pattern to cite. However, at the secondary level the past practice in many dioceses was to have a diocesan priest serve as the principal of the school. In those instances where a woman religious was appointed principal, the usual practice was for the bishop to appoint a priest as director, coordinator, or school pastor. The intent of that practice was to provide clear lines of canonical authority. In many dioceses, this is no longer the practice with the result that the issue of authority is not as clear. In some instances, boards have been constituted as, or have assumed the position of being, jurisdictional or policymaking. In other schools, the principal functions almost autonomously. Neither of these extremes is desirable. If diocesan schools are to remain tied to the diocese canonically, there has to be clear lines of accountability and responsibility. Before attempting to determine these lines, it is important for the diocese to state how it wants to relate to these schools. For instance if the bishop through the school office wishes to establish or maintain a close tie in with the principal of each school and the size of the diocese permits it, the superintendent of schools could be designated as that person to whom the principal is directly responsible. In this instance the principal would be hired by the superintendent in much the same way that the pastor hires the principal of the parish school.

The same guidelines and norms governing roles and relationships would apply. On the other hand, in complex situations, the diocesan school could be erected as a juridic person in its own right. In those cases the principal would become the canonical administrator of the school and accountable to the bishop for the administration of the goods and services of the school. The advantage of this model is that the school functions as a separate juridic person with specific rights and responsibilities as given in the Code of Canon Law.

Regardless of which model the diocese uses, the role of the school board remains an issue. Recognizing that boards are currently functioning with differing understandings and differing degrees of "authority," the challenge of sharing responsibility for the operations of the diocesan school remains. Whether school boards have been operating for a number of years, are relatively new, or are non existent, diocesan officials need to ask themselves as well as the people in the field: Why should we have school boards? What can they do that is not or cannot be done by the professional educators? Without clarity about these basic questions, no organizational model will make sense in the long run. After the initial enthusiasm wears off, the group itself will spend time trying to answer these very same questions. Although it may be appropriate for each group to define itself in terms of specific long-range goals, it is not the responsibility of each board to determine its authority and/or how it will relate to the diocese.

Perhaps the most commonly asked question regarding the constitution of boards is: Are they policymaking? What is meant by this term varies. For some dioceses, the practice is for the boards to meet, make decisions, and have them either ratified or vetoed by someone in authority. Because the practice of veto is rarely used, the boards appear to have the final authority. As long as all is going well, no one has problems. However, when there is disagreement about direction, personnel, and finances, then the issue of authority arises with resulting hostility and annimosity. For an institution which has the building of community as one of its prime purposes to allow this kind of situation to develop or continue is, at best, inappropriate. Unless the bishop is willing to allow the school to function as a separate incorporation with a board of trustees which has jurisdiction over the operation of the school (with the understanding that the bishop retains authority over the religious education and catholicity), then the diocese must clarify the issue of who in fact has authority in what areas in diocesan schools. A case could be made for a number of approaches. However, it does not seem realistic to attempt to constitute a school board for a diocesan school in a manner which does not recognize the already defined and operative authority structure of the Church. Boards can be organized in a manner which recognize that fact and give parents and other concerned parties a responsible voice in the operation of Catholic schools.

INTERPARISH SCHOOLS

Because the trend toward the formation of an increasing number of interparish/regional/consolidated schools is growing, the governance and accountability practices regarding these schools need particular attention. At the present time, they constitute 17.8 percent of the Catholic schools; 6.4 percent are elementary and 11.4 percent are secondary.[7] Whatever challenges face the Catholic educational community regarding parish, diocesan, and private schools, they pale in comparision to the problems of interparish schools.

Even if in practice the governance issues of other schools lack clarity, at least it is clear who has the authority. How that individual chooses to exercise the authority is not the issue here. In a parish school, the principal is accountable to the pastor; in a private school, to the major superior and council of the religious congregation through whatever structure they have established; in a diocesan school to the bishop usually through the superintendent of schools. Given the organization of those schools which are designated as interparish, a major problem occurs when there is no one who has the canonical authority for the school. Some of these schools attempt to function with the pastors of the contributing parishes assuming this position. Ordinarily this approach is workable as long as the individuals who were involved in the original reorganization remain. Because this arrangement is largely dependent on personalities rather than sound organizational principles, it does not provide a firm foundation for the future.

The vacuum created when the locus of authority is absent is frequently filled by a strong principal who more often than not operates in an independent and often quite successful manner. In the absence of such a leader, the board which finds itself in the position of having to function in a manner which can blur the distinctions between policy and administration and often creates problems regarding responsibilities for policies. In this situation the person who has to deal with the everyday realities of this situation is the principal.

Often it is not clear to whom the principal is formally accountable and as a result, she or he ends up answering to many different individuals and groups as if they had formal authority. Even if an individual principal with special fortitude could sustain this ambivalent situation, the lack of clarity serves as a deterrent to the future of the school. For instance, in many of these schools, responsibility for the property which is used by the school is not clearly defined. Probably the site is one which formerly functioned as a parish school and technically is still "owned" by that parish. Now that the responsibility for the school is shared with other parishes, who assumes this role? Often the interparish school board finds itself functioning as if it were the group responsible or the founding parish finds itself maintaining the buildings without a systematic means of sharing this burden with the other contributing parishes.

While more and more dioceses are developing guidelines in this regard, there seems to be a pressing need to clarify the status of these schools. This governance issue is current because the number of these schools is increasing. More and more dioceses are working with parishes toward mergers and consolidations necessitated by population shifts. If the "new" schools are supported by more than one parish, they are indeed regional schools. It is important to discover some method of organizing this type of school so that the relationship with the institutional church is clear. If a school is going to call itself Catholic, the bishop has responsibility to insure his relationship with and commitment to the future strength of the school. One model already functioning in practice if not by policy is that of the school's being erected as a juridic person.

There are interparish schools with boards which have begun to assume a role similar to that of the juridic person. Many have assumed debts in the name of the interparish school or board; others have sued or been sued in a court of law. Often the school's relationships are not formalized and in some instances the school seems to have all of the responsibilities and none of the rights of a juridic person in church law.

At the beginning of this chapter, it was suggested that what really happens in the governance and accountability of Catholic schools is largely dependent on the personalities, politics, and policies present at the local level. This is the real situation. However, this comment need not be construed in a negative manner. There is a tremendous amount of goodwill, leadership, and conviction regarding the value and potential of Catholic schools today. Those in leadership positions have the obligation to address the issues involved in governance and accountability in some systematic manner. Principals of Catholic schools and board members are competent, dedicated individuals who share a vision of what Catholic schools are for the church and society. They alone cannot resolve these issues. The real tragedy will occur if people of goodwill who share responsibility for the post-Vatican II church allow local politics to prevent their addressing these issues. Years ago, a wise statesman reminded us that often evil prevails when good people do nothing. This statement should not be true of Catholic educational leaders today.

SUMMARY

1. Catholic schools are usually organized under four structures: parish, interparish, diocesan, and private. The policies and practices of governance and accountability in them are varied and unique to local circumstances.
2. Parish schools, at least in theory, have clear lines of authority. The key to successful administration is for the principal to determine how to work with the pastor, the canonical authority of the parish and the parish council, as well as with the numerous school communities to which the principal owes accountability. A key issue in these relations is who hires the principal.
3. While the lines of authority remain clear as far as ownership and sponsorship of private Catholic schools are concerned, there seems to be a changing climate regarding the schools' operations. Religious congregations need to be clear in establishing expectations and relationships with the school's board of directors/trustees.
4. A diocese needs to determine its relationship with those schools designated as diocesan. Regardless of the organizational model in place, the role of the school board remains an issue. Recognizing that boards are currently functioning with differing understandings and degrees of "authority," the challenge of sharing responsibility for the operations of the diocesan school remains.
5. Given the organization of those schools which are designated as interparish, a major problem occurs when there is no one who has the canonical authority for the school. Because the number of interparish schools is increasing, this governance issue is critical and some means of organizing this type of school so that the relationship with the institutional church is clear must be determined.
6. Catholic school personnel, especially those in leadership positions, must address the current issues involved in governance and accountability in some systematic manner.

FOOTNOTES

1. *United States Catholic Elementary and Secondary Schools, 1984-1985* (Washington, D.C.: National Catholic Educational Association, 1985), p. 10.

2. *The Code of Canon Law* (Grand Rapids, Michigan: Wm. B. Eerdmans Publishing Company, 1983), Book V, Title II.

3. Rev. John A. Gilbert, *Pastor As Shepherd of the School Community* (Washington, D.C.: National Catholic Educational Association,

1983).

4. *Effective Catholic Schools: An Exploration* (Washington, D.C.: National Center for Research in Total Catholic Education, 1984).

5. *United States Catholic Elementary and Secondary Schools 1984-1985,* op. cit.

6. *Ibid.*

7. *Ibid.*

SUGGESTED READINGS

Mallett, Rev. James K. "Reflections on the Application of the New Code of Canon Law to the Governance of Catholic Educational Institutions." A clear and concise presentation to the 1985 St. Louis NCEA Convention which offers, among other topics, suggestions to Catholic education leaders regarding board models.

Sheehan, Sr. Lourdes. "Catholic Boards Must Recognize the Authority Structure," *Momentum.* Washington, DC: National Catholic Educational Association, February, 1985, pp. 32-33. Offers suggestions as to reasons why some boards have experienced difficulty functioning.

CHAPTER II
PERSONNEL SELECTION
by Medard Shea, C.F.X., M.Ed.

Presently Deputy Superintendent in the Office of Catholic Education in the Diocese of Brooklyn, Brother Shea was in charge of teacher personnel for eight years. A former high school teacher and principal, he has written and spoken on this subject around the country.

THE CATHOLIC SCHOOL TEACHER

Catholic schools are value oriented schools. In the Pre-Vatican II era, not only were the vast majority of teachers members of religious orders whose religious habits and absolute dedication to Catholicity were reflected in every facet of school operation, but the teaching of religion itself was based upon unchanging doctrine, catechism, and formal discipline.

Since Vatican II almost every above-mentioned element of Catholic schools has undergone both scrutiny and change. The majority of the teaching staff today are lay teachers. The religious habit has undergone radical change with the majority of religious teachers assuming secular garb. The teaching of religion has moved far from the formalized, rigid programs of the past. Society has become more complex and demanding. The Catholic teacher of today, lay or religious, must meet the demands of the present era of change and unrest. Vatican II opened a new era in Catholic education necessitating a complete re-education of all teachers. The job of teaching in a Catholic school requires not only a spiritual and personal dedication to the service of teaching, but an updated understanding and knowledge of the church in today's world.

The Catholic teacher today faces a formidable task. Family support is much weakened, and in many cases almost non-existent. The knowledge explosion of the past decades places tremendous demands on teachers; and the influence of technology on youth puts teachers in competing roles with other media for education. The Catholicity of the schools is the responsibility of the administrators and teachers. Church documents speak of teachers who demonstrate ''an integrated approach to learning and living" and who "integrate culture and faith." Teachers who take this integrated approach will work well in a Catholic school.

If a school, as a distinctive educational community, involves administration and faculty, parents and pupils in the common purpose of communicating Catholic faith and tradition, it can truly be called Catholic. Teachers have said, "It doesn't matter what I believe. I don't teach religion. I teach math." This attitude points up sharply the need for teacher training programs in Catholic schools. It also points up the need to inform teacher candidates before they are hired why the Catholic school exists, plus the obligation of teachers in a Catholic school to know, practice, and teach Catholicism in all aspects of the school program. The Catholic school is unique, with specific goals and purposes; and every staff member must be aware of and contribute to this uniqueness.

People continue to ask "Can a Catholic school be Catholic with a lay staff." The answer is a resounding "Yes"! However, there are other questions on selecting, hiring, personal characteristics, working conditions, salaries, social justice, teacher preparation, teacher competencies that must also be considered. The United States Catholic bishops have taken a leadership role in defining the Catholic school. The pastoral *To Teach as Jesus Did* has become the cornerstone for building a faith community in a Catholic school. Later the role of the Catholic school teacher was specifically defined in the Vatican document *The Catholic School:*

"By their witness and their behavior teachers are of the first importance to impart a distinctive character to Catholic schools. It is, therefore, indispensable to ensure their continuing formation through some form of suitable pastoral provision. This must aim to animate them as witnesses of Christ in the classroom and tackle the problems of their particular apostolate, especially regarding a Christian vision of the world and of teaching in accordance with the principles of the Gospel."[1]

The ultimate rationale for a program of Christian formation of teachers can be summed up in one phrase: "that teachers practice what they preach." The ultimate result is most explicitly stated in the Vatican's *Declaration on Christian Formation:*

"But let teachers realize that to the greatest possible extent they determine whether the Catholic school can bring its goals and undertakings to fruition. They should, therefore, be trained with particular care so that they may be enriched with both secular and religious knowledge, appropriately certified, and may be equipped with an educational skill which reflects modern-day findings. Bound by charity to one another and to their students, and penetrated by an apostolic spirit, let them give witness to Christ, the unique Teacher, by their lives as well as by their teachings."[2]

While teachers in their daily efforts in the classroom bring about the goals and objectives of the Catholic philosophy, the responsibility also belongs to school administrators. Personnel selection, training, and supervision are the key elements of administrative leadership in attaining the goals of Catholic education. A Catholic school must not only turn out well-educated students, but also well-educated Catholic students.

The teacher in the classroom is the front line for achieving this goal of a well-educated Catholic student. Catholic administrators at all levels must insure that this Catholic teacher is well qualified and able to carry out his or her teaching duties in a responsible manner.

Along with all of the efforts to provide teachers with the skills and knowledge to be good instructors is the need to provide teachers with adequate working conditions, salary and benefits which fulfill the church's teaching on labor and social justice. To this end there is the need to provide administrators with the knowledge, guidance and direction necessary for teacher personnel relations in Catholic schools.

TEACHER ORGANIZATIONS AND ALTERNATIVES

Administrators in the pre-Vatican II era had an easy time, from one viewpoint, in what are today termed personnel relations in Catholic schools. Religious principals, who were often also the community superiors, directed their religious staff according to congregational practices, rules, and guidelines.

Religious teachers were assigned to schools according to need, talents and abilities. They were also mobile. Aside from routine transfers by the congregation, personality conflicts, administrative problems, or classroom problems could be resolved with transfers. This element of mobility of both administrators and teachers was one means of resolving personnel issues.

Such mobility barely exists for today's religious staffers and is not a significant factor at all for the primarily lay-staffed Catholic schools. This limited lay staff mobility is a major factor in the intense and personal interest of lay teachers in improving their working conditions. Aside from the basic differences in life style between a religious and a lay teacher, this local orientation contributes strongly to the growth and development of teacher organizations of various types to improve and change personnel practices.

Recently personnel operations entered a new era as teachers challenged church leaders to practice the "social justice" they preached. There is no question that a decade ago both sides, church leaders and teacher groups, moved awkwardly in the unfamiliar territory of "labor relations." Controversy, confrontation and a negative press were the norm as both sides struggled to seek a peaceful, practical and just solution to what were difficult issues.

Great progress has been made. The times are more peaceful and cooperative relationships now exist in most dioceses. The frequent teacher strikes of the 1970's are less frequent. Differing opinions of what constitutes "social justice" in labor relations remain.

When Catholic teachers first began organizing in the late 1960's, they had one model for labor relations, a national union model suitable for industry. Even then, teachers used the word "association" rather than "union" in their organizational titles.

Church leaders, while accepting and even encouraging such organizing, were upset and uncertain as to how to work with and react to the adversary relationships of these groups. Obviously, the church should be a leader in the area of good labor relations. As Msgr. George Higgins challenged: "administrators of Catholic institutions should strike out on their own and, for once, take the lead in establishing progressive labor-management relations in their particular profession..."[3]

Previously affiliated with the AFT, many teacher unions have withdrawn from that organization. Most have now affiliated with the National Association of Catholic School Teachers (NACST) based in Philadelphia. This group is very active in recruiting affiliates in Catholic dioceses. NACST stresses the Catholic aspect of its operation; the need and importance of Catholic schools; and indicates a willingness to work with alternative methods of bargaining.

Among the alternatives to straight union-style bargaining is the "non-confrontational, win/win method" of negotiation. In this method, negotiations are carried out in an atmosphere of trust and cooperation, coming to an agreement acceptable to both parties, and precluding the concept that one side or the other must "win" at the negotiating table.

John Augenstein has written *A Collaborative Approach to Personnel Relations*,[4] a model process for justice in the Catholic school community of faith. This document is filled with advice and counsel to meet the needs of both administrators and teachers in reaching consensus in personnel relations.

Beyond the area of organized associations with broad membership, procedures and dues, there is another type of association of teachers, those organized as a bargaining association in individual schools. These are definitely not "company unions" as the impetus for organizing and selecting spokespersons comes as much from administration as from the teachers themselves. This type of in-school association is successful in larger high schools with large lay staffs, but could work in any school with a high percentage of lay teachers.

As a rule, these groups have been successful in asserting teacher rights, working conditions, benefits and salaries, while rarely becoming militant. Administrators also find such in-school associations beneficial in the personnel area of school administration. Teacher unions are intimately related to personnel practices. Poor personnel practices provide a fertile ground for union organizers, who will zero in on disgruntled unhappy teachers.

The church stresses the rights of workers to organize. Morally, unionization cannot be opposed and should even be supported. However, there is a right to be cautious about the aims and purposes of particular unions who would organize Catholic teachers. The encyclicals recommend organizing to obtain proper, due rights of workers. Catholic administrators should provide and foster these conditions in the first place without the impetus of third parties.

CONTRACTS/AGREEMENTS AND APPLICATION

Webster's dictionary defines contract as a binding agreement between two parties. Never was so much implied in so few words! Teacher contracts are either written or unwritten. For the sake of good personnel practice, every teacher should have a written contract. There are enough legal pitfalls with written contracts without considering the untold complications possible in an unwritten agreement.

Teachers today are well aware of their legal rights. With government agencies and regulations in the areas of human rights, equal opportunity employment, due process, state and national labor boards, plus the nationwide tendency to file suit for every real or fancied fault, the need for written agreements (contracts) is absolutely necessary.

Teacher contracts vary widely, from simple statements of dates and salaries to the inclusion of detailed working conditions, church law, legal obligations, and more. An administrator should put no more in writing than is absolutely necessary. At the same time, the administrator should put in writing everything deemed important and/or necessary. A contract binds both parties. But what happens when either party breaches the contract? What, for example, happens when a teacher walks out on a contract while simply notifying or in some cases not notifying the principal? What recourse is available to the principal? Little or no punitive action is available.

Legal action for breach of contract is fruitless. Some dioceses have a penalty clause in dollars for such a breach, but it is unenforceable for the most part. It may, however, make a teacher think twice before breaking the contract. Depending upon circumstances, a non-recommendation may be made part of the teacher's file. A breach of contract by the principal is something else entirely. Every element of the contract binds administration. It may not be equal justice, but it is fact. Government agencies are available to a teacher who believes that his or her contractual rights have been violated. If a teacher union is the signer of the contract the issue will probably become more complex. The third and only uncomplicated breaking of a contract is by mutual agreement of the parties concerned. It is recommended that such a mutual agreement be in writing and signed by both parties. Good administration of contracted personnel demands consistency. The following words and phrases refer to good personnel practices:

1. *Consistency*—no *ad hoc* operation. Treat all similar situations in the same fashion.
2. *In writing*—anything important enough to be needed for future reference should be put in writing, dated, signed and filed.
3. *Precedent*—be aware and beware of exceptions to working conditions. They can quickly become the rule.
4. *"I'll get back to you."*—a key phrase when you are presented with a difficult or tricky decision. Better a delay for a proper decision, than a quick, hurried wrong decision.
5. *Equal and fair treatment*—understand that both cannot apply in every case. Consider how an administrator should treat a beginning teacher and a veteran teacher differently.
6. *Don't be kind to teachers*—more problems in principal/teacher relationships result from "kindness" than anything else. "Kindness" inappropriately applied has a way of bending rules and regulations and upsetting morale. Be pleasant, sociable, honest, fair, and

open, but treat teachers as responsible, mature persons.

As is evident, in today's world the principal must be familiar with good personnel practices, beginning with the guidelines, rights, responsibilities and restrictions of the contract/agreement. A good teacher contract/agreement, mutually negotiated, carefully administered, and respected by both parties, is reasonable assurance of a successful school operation.

THE DILEMMA OF TEACHER SALARIES

Probably one of the most troublesome issues in Catholic schools today is the issue of salaries. Though great efforts are being made, Catholic teacher salaries are generally well below the salaries of their public school counterparts. Other factors beyond salary make teaching in Catholic schools attractive to new and veteran teachers alike, but decisions on teaching most often come down to salary. Moreover, there is little doubt that many qualified, capable dedicated Catholic teachers leave Catholic schools annually for much better salaries in business, industry and public schools.

Can Catholic schools meet this salary challenge? There is no easy answer. The church teaches that a laborer is worthy of a just wage. But where are financially strapped Catholic schools going to find the money needed?

Catholic school administrators, bishops, pastors, principals and parents must face this salary dilemma. Is a teacher's salary based upon what a school can afford, even if it is well below a "just wage"? If a teacher will work for a low wage, is justice being served? Are some Catholic schools, unable to pay a living wage, facing the more serious question of whether they can function only by practicing injustice to their employees? A hard question indeed!

It is evident that most Catholic schools, especially parish schools, will not be able to compete with the market place in terms of salaries. However, they should at least pay a living wage. What this living wage is varies from city to city, area to area, but administrators should have a good concept of a living wage at their location and strive to pay it.

Whim, past practice and guesswork should not be the foundations for a salary scale. Careful planning, good budgeting and the guidance of social justice are basic building blocks to a living wage. Every school should have a published salary scale for its teachers.

Since teacher salaries are as high as 85 percent of a school budget, tuition, fund raising and parish support must be used to meet this need. For the most part, parents are unaware of the salaries paid to teachers or the impact of salaries on tuition rates. Parents are often shocked to learn that teacher salaries are well below their own salaries. Schools should publish teacher salary scales. The fear of losing students because of increased tuitions will be allayed to some extent because parents are more willing to pay a just, living wage, once they know the facts.

The issue of going public, being open, is the key factor. Teachers need to know the financial facts of a school's operation, to make judgments as to what is available for salaries. Closed financial books are a prime source of discord in negotiations. The old myth that the bishop (pastor) is sitting on a gold mine has to be disproved. The myth persists that there is money somewhere. Only financial openness will eliminate this myth and open the door to realistic negotiation.

A corollary to the salary issue is benefits. Pension, medical benefits, and FICA costs can range from 20 to 25 percent of a teacher's salary and most teachers and many administrators are unaware of this added cost. Normally, teachers take such benefits for granted and do not consider benefits as part of salary. Administrators must be aware of these added costs in negotiating salaries.

Teacher salaries and attendant issues, benefits, recruitment, retention, and the like, are a major concern of Catholic schools. If Catholic education is to continue to thrive in the future, these concerns must be faced now. Government assistance, such as tuition tax credits, is a real need; but if and when it comes, it will only assist schools, not alleviate the current problem.

CHANGED TEACHING STAFFS

Catholic schools nationwide have just ended an era of largely religious order staffing and changed to a strongly lay staffed operation. This trend began in the late sixties, moved rapidly in the seventies, and is a reality today. With the changes in society, the effects of Vatican II on the church and the great national emphasis on education, a whole new era in Catholic education is here.

Just look at Catholic schools today compared to ten and twenty years ago. From a system that in many places was made up of more than 90 to 95 percent of its administrators and teachers from religious communities, it has changed to a system of education with 80 percent of its teaching staff made up of lay teachers. With this change has come the need to review and radically revise the ordinary religious congregation personnel practices. Up to the late 1960's there existed a pattern of principal/superiors as administrators of Catholic schools. The line of administration and teaching was based on the traditions and patterns of religious communities. School operations were based on the educational principles and practices of the religious community.

Today, however, the positions of religious superior and principal are often separated. Just as the superior's role is much changed in religious life, so is the role of principal, lay or religious, in the school. Ordinary paper work has reached monumental proportions, as Catholic schools have become more professional and as state and federal educational agencies have made increased demands upon principals. The greatest change, however, has come in staffing. The proportion of lay staff is growing greater every year, both from a dearth of vocations to religious life, the retirement of active religious, and the movement to other Christian works outside the classroom by religious.

In the face of this change in staffing there still exists an administrative pattern that is geared to religious-staffed schools. The traditional pattern of operation of many religious orders still influences the day-to-day administration in Catholic schools. In most cases, this is all for the best. In some, it is close to disastrous, as administrators fail to move into the era of the lay-oriented school. There is an awareness that times have changed, but patterns of decades of religious administration are difficult to overcome and change comes slowly.

There are two observations that flow from this situation. First, the distinction between lay and religious teachers is not as pronounced as it used to be; both work side-by-side, almost indistinguishable, particularly where dress no longer sets one apart from the other. Second, the changes in life style of many religious communities further blurs distinctions as far as working conditions are concerned.

All of these developments reveal the influence lay personnel have in Catholic schools as both administrators and teachers. Early fears that Catholic schools could not and would not survive without the religious teachers have proved to be mostly unfounded. Catholic schools with all lay staffs or predominently lay staffs are living up to and continuing traditions of Catholicity and academic excellence common to Catholic education in the past.

Religious congregations whose primary service was to schools have continued to serve and to staff them (to the extent possible) but with fewer numbers. In general, they have assisted, cooperated with, and encouraged lay personnel to work and administer Catholic schools.

One significant change which resulted from the diminished ratio of religious to lay personnel was that the school supervisory role of religious congregations also diminished and has in fact generally disappeared. Diocesan school/education offices have moved into this supervisory role by increasing their supervisory and curriculum services which were formerly the province of the religious congregation which staffed the school.

This same process of change on the diocesan office level led to the growth and greater influence and direction from religious education offices. Programs from the Department of Chief Administrators of Catholic Education of the National Catholic Educational Association recognized this need for religious education early and much was done and is still being done in the realm of religious education and catechetics in Catholic schools. Many pastors reluctantly accepted lay administrators for their parish schools, feeling that parents wanted a religious as principal. Having no religious available forced schools to hire lay staff. Pastors have been pleasantly surprised to find that well-educated, dedicated, and competent lay teachers proved to be excellent principals.

Parents are also very much aware of the impact of lay staff on Catholic schools. By their involvement in the schools they have indicated that the schools are providing the kind of Catholic education they want for their children. Since great financial sacrifices are called for, parental support for Catholic education is one of the surest signs that current lay oriented Catholic schooling is successful. Probably more than in any other area of the changing church, lay influence, leadership, and participation is equal to or greater in the Catholic schools than in any other area of church ministry.

THE MARKET FOR TEACHER CANDIDATES

The market for teacher candidates for Catholic schools varies widely from city to city from state to state. The need for teachers has increased in all school systems, even as the number of pupils has decreased nationally. In the larger dioceses, Catholic schools are having particular difficulty in finding good teacher candidates. One reason for the limited number of teacher candidates is the loss of prestige for the teaching profession, reflected in the very low percentage of college students planning on a teaching career.

Catholic administrators have a further problem in seeking candidates from this limited pool of teacher prospects. First, Catholic administrators want and prefer Catholic candidates, though necessity dictates a relaxing of this requirement. Second, an overriding problem is that the salaries offered in most Catholic schools are in competition with much higher public school salaries. Though recent studies have shown a steady increase in salary scales for Catholic school teachers on the elementary level, these salaries are, in general, well below the public school scale. In addition, there is a nationwide clamor to increase greatly public school salaries, a prospect that will add to the Catholic school salary problem. Still, there are a great number of teacher candidates who prefer to teach in Catholic schools. Salary is not always the determining factor in their decision to teach in a particular school system.

Increasing salaries and benefits, plus increasingly lay staffs are placing a great financial burden on parish schools. Social justice demands a living wage for teachers, even as many parishes are undergoing a very limited growth in income. These factors all influence teacher recruitment: the supply of candidates, their church relationship, the salary level and the parish financial situation. Teacher recruitment has become the number one priority of personnel directors and administrators. Seeking capable, well-trained, Catholic candidates is the prime task. Recruitment requires a positive program of advertisement and personal effort. College and university campuses are the major source of teacher prospects. Personal visits to students in their sophomore and junior years are recommended to make known the opportunities and satisfaction to be found in teaching in Catholic schools. These visits should include non-denominational colleges as well as Catholic colleges. Most colleges will post flyers about opportunities for teaching in Catholic schools.

In both Catholic and secular newspapers and magazines, ads are another sources of teacher applications. No area of advertising and promotion should be overlooked including announcements in parish bulletins.

A positive attitude about the rewards and satisfaction to be found in teaching in a Catholic school should be stressed. Thousands of Catholic school graduates are in colleges and universities, most with fond memories of their previous Catholic education. Many need only to be reminded that they are welcome and needed as teachers in these same schools that taught them.

FACTORS IN TEACHER INTERVIEWS

The most important event in personnel practice is the teacher applicant interview. Careless, shallow interviews fail to detect potential future difficulties. Careful, in-depth interviews provide some assurance of future success. Although not infallible, a positive interview process will certainly eliminate many problems before they have a chance to develop.

A teacher application form is a primary requisite in the hiring process. Practically every diocese has such a form which complies with national and local restrictions. Copies are available in every diocese. Once this form has been received by the school, the first decision can be made, namely, whether or not this applicant should or should not be interviewed.

If the applicant has previous teaching experience, it is vitally important to check with the present or former employer as to the applicant's status, whether satisfactory or not. An important question to ask a current or former employer is "Will or would you rehire this person?" After the application is completed properly, the next step is to set the interview date, which in a school situation might include a demonstration lesson on site as part of the interview process.

The interview time should be at the convenience of the interviewer, not vice versa. Depending upon the school situation, a second person may also be scheduled to interview the applicant in the scheduled time frame.

Wherever the interview takes place, it should provide privacy. The structure of the interview should be well prepared. The school philosophy is of major importance and should be explained. Salary and working conditions are obvious elements. The interviewees should be given ample opportunity both to react and to explain their qualifications and their own goals as teachers in a Catholic school. An interview that does not give applicants a chance to answer more than yes or no to questions is very limited. The interviewer should share the time and conversation in order to make a valid judgment about the personal qualities of the person interviewed.

Note taking during an interview may prove to be valuable. Or the interviewer may summarize the interview after the candidate departs. It is important to know the candidate's decision about accepting the position before the school sends notice of its decision. The candidate's decision can be learned as part of the interview or shortly thereafter in writing. Then, the school can state its decision.

The entire process is important, but how the applicant follows instructions is a valuable indication as to how the applicant will act in a working situation. In an emergency, where interview procedures must be bypassed, some form of temporary hiring should be used until credentials are properly checked.

A summary of an interview or screening process should include the following elements.

- professional and academic competence
- basic knowledge of the applicant's public and private life
- understanding of the philosophy of the school
- participation in religious activities of the school
- working conditions of this particular school
- knowledge that public violation of church teachings is grounds for dismissal
- demonstration lesson

A proper interview will go a long way towards the development of a workable, successful school operation.

HIRING TEACHERS: PRACTICES AND PRECAUTIONS

Presuming that a supply of teacher candidates is available, the priority question becomes the hiring procedure. Casual or careless hiring procedures are a definite invitation to future headaches and problems. Firing rhymes with hiring and poor hiring inevitable leads to troublesome firing.

The NCEA recognized this situation and as early as 1973 set up a committee to develop guidelines. This committee quickly realized that it could not come up with absolute infallible and complete guidelines in this relatively unexplored new area. "Guidelines" became the key word as the committee developed a beginning framework (still valid) upon which different school systems in all parts of the nation could select and develop what was most useful to their particular aims and goals.

The basic framework for these guidelines covered three areas: selecting teachers from among a group of applicants; outlining basic principles which all teachers would be expected to believe in, follow, and practice; and setting up standards on growth and development of teachers in service in theschools.

The following is from the set of guidelines called: *Procedures for Selection of Teachers for Catholic Schools*

A) Application Process

25

1. Include questions on the role of teachers in the purposes and uniqueness of Catholic schools.
2. In the collection of factual data, be aware of limitations by the Equal Opportunity Commission on certain information.
3. Obtain information on academic background and credentials; accept only official transcripts.
4. Include a statement by the applicant as to the accuracy of the information, for example, "I understand that any misrepresentation of facts in this application will be considered just cause for dismissal at the discretion of the employer."
5. Ask permission to investigate any of the facts or statements submitted, for example, "I hereby grant _____ permission to investigate any of the facts or statements submitted by me, except where my written statement upon this form specifically requests that no investigation be made."
6. Indicate on the application the length of time you will file the application if the person is not hired.
7. Check with previous employers.
8. If the applicant is an ex-religious, contact the former congregation; let the applicant suggest one person and you select another.
9. Be sensitive to the problems caused by last minute or panic hiring procedures.

B) Interview Process
1. All documents and materials (references and transcripts) should be on file before the interview is conducted. Realize that it may not be possible to obtain information from present employer.
2. During the interview respect the confidentiality of information submitted regarding the applicant.
3. Interview questions and discussions should focus on "Guiding Principles for Teacher Commitment in Light of the pastoral *To Teach as Jesus Did*" and "Guidelines for Teachers in Catholic Schools."
4. More than one person should interview the applicant (both at central office level and at the local school level).
5. Make notes as soon after the interview as possible. Be honest; include both strengths and weaknesses of the applicant.
6. If possible, the interview process should provide for observation of applicant in classroom situation.

C) Orientation Program
1. In order to avoid conflicts between theory and practice, build

the program around the "Guiding Principles for Teacher Commitment in Light of the Pastoral *To Teach as Jesus Did*" and "Guidelines for Teachers in Catholic Schools." Words and witness must be harmonized in order to avoid ambiguity.

These procedures are very basic but necessary. Certainly they are the minimum guidelines for teacher hiring. They present a set of positive steps to which each diocese or school might add or expand for its own specific conditions.

There are some negative factors or caution in hiring. If the applicant has previous teaching experience, it is mandatory that the principal contact the previous employer before making a commitment. The applicant may already be under contract or may have been terminated for cause by the previous employer. So called "off the street" or "panic" hiring is always risky.

A substantial part of the interview should be concerned with the applicant's understanding and acceptance of the philosophy of the Catholic school and the public observance of the laws of the church. When a school has a stated philosophy which can actually be seen in practice in the day-to-day operation of the school, the administrator has an instrument upon which to base his or her judgments about the suitability of a prospective teacher to join the staff. This assumes that the prospective teacher has already been found competent and desirable in the academic framework of the school.

The last step in the process for selection of a teacher is the decision to hire or not to hire an individual. It need not be hurried and is best done in writing within and agreed upon, specified period. The administrator then has time to digest the interview, seek information, if such is needed, and come to a considered decision. If hired, the applicant should be requested or refused in writing.

Finally, the hiring decision from among professionally qualified and eligible candidates should make the Christian dimension of the individual a priority consideration. The candidate should clearly understand the minimum expectations as regards beliefs, attitudes, and behaviors. There should be no surprises on either side once the candidate reports for work.

Alfred McBride has written: "Hiring a believer does not guarantee the enduring commitment of the believer. The powers of secularization in the culture are sufficiently seductive and enchanting to the point that they may prevail over our Catholic educators and weaken their dedication to Christ. . . .Catholic educators need the life-long possibilities of the grace of evangelization, the loving summons to a firm commitment of Jesus."[5]

THE NON-CATHOLIC EDUCATOR IN A CATHOLIC SCHOOL

Previously mentioned guidelines have implicitly been directed to to the hiring of Catholic teachers. The issue of both non-Catholic teachers and students in Catholic schools is an unresolved challenge to the schools.

In *The Christian Formation of Catholic Educators*, Alfred McBride applies his seven guidelines for Catholic educators to non-Catholic educators in Catholic schools. He notes that his comments and guidelines "are brief and tentative because of the complexity of the situation and its comparative newness in Catholic schools."[6]

His brief introduction to the seven guidelines is as compact an overview of the non-Catholic teacher situation as can be found and deserves repetition here as a conclusion to this teacher hiring section:

"The preceding seven guidelines concern the Christian Formation of Catholic educators. What is to be said about non-Catholic educators teaching in our Catholic schools? In some cases they constitute as much as a third of our elementary and secondary school faculties. While most of them are Protestant Christians, some are Jews, humanists and of other religio-philosophical persuasions. Correspondingly, there are cases where a significant number of the students are non-Catholics. What can we do to help non-Catholic educators support the Catholic Christian goals of our schools, while retaining their own integrity and personal beliefs?

"The answers are not simple, partly due to the wide range of belief systems involved and the necessary respect and reverence due to those of differing persuasions. The first step must be to hire only those persons who agree to support the philosophy and goals of the school. At the outset, the principal should review clearly what the school expects of the educator. If the candidate has a conscience problem with what the school expects, then he or she should not be hired—nor even propose to accept the job. Honesty and frankness at the outset is of the essence.

"On the positive side, let it be said that many principals report deep satisfaction with their non Catholic faculty members, finding them to be exceptionally sincere in advancing the religious nature of the school and energetic in maintaining its moral tone."[7]

AFFIRMATIVE ACTION

Affirmative action is a term with many ramifications. Fundamentally, it means that there can be no discrimination in hiring due to race, color, creed or sex. It implies not only the negative aspect of avoiding discrimination, but positive efforts to overcome and make up for past discrimination. The Catholic Church throughout history has been the church of all nationalities, truly universal in its membership and its service to all people.

Where does affirmative action fit into local Catholic school situations today? A first instance would be in personnel practices. Teacher applicants are considered without prejudice as to race, color and sex. Note the "creed" is omitted, since religion is a specific consideration in Catholic schools.

Legally consideration of the religion of a teacher applicant is the one exception permitted for Catholic schools. Administrators have the right to question the religious beliefs of prospective teachers for a Catholic school. They cannot discriminate on the other areas of affirmative action, but can definitely inquire, question and make decisions based upon the Catholicity of an applicant. In cases where the applicant is a non-Catholic, the administrator still has the right to insure that the applicant has the moral values which are looked for in a teacher in a Catholic school. Such candidates can be rejected on the grounds that their beliefs or religious practices are not acceptable for a teacher in a Catholic classroom.

In the same vein, it is also evident that some Catholic applicants may have unacceptable attitudes towards church teachings and practices, which would be considered more harmful than good in the classroom. Again, these are legal grounds for rejection or non-hiring. At all times, the goals and purposes of a Catholic school are paramount and this very Catholicity is the key element in selecting teachers.

Proper use of the school's philosophy will be a proper guide for moral and religious decisions in the hiring process, presuming that other personal and academic qualifications are met. There is no question but that a teacher in a Catholic school must first of all accept the philosophy of the school wholeheartedly, be a good example to the students, and cooperate in every way with the Catholic nature of the institution.

CAPSULES OF CHANGE

Yesterday—1940-60
1. Parish supported school
2. No tuition charged
3. Entire parish paid for school operation
4. Fund raising—parish activity
5. School/parish fiscal accounts combined
6. Buildings in generally good condition
7. No government aid
8. All religious principals
9. 95-100% religious faculty
10. Religious lived in parish convent
11. Few, no non-Catholics
12. Every Catholic child expected automatically to attend
13. Ethnic solidarity
14. Class size large—40 and higher
15. Self-contained classes
16. All children basically capable of learning
17. Most students from two-parent families
18. Few kindergartens
19. No nursery schools
20. Policy—basically pastoral
21. No civic community activity
22. CCD—responsibility of school principal
23. Most schools/parishes saw themselves as an island

Today—1980-85
1. Parish carries an ever smaller percentage of school operation costs
2. Escalating tuition rates
3. Stress on parents only paying tuition
4. Separate fund raising by school/parents
5. School budget separate from parish budget
6. Major maintenance required in many buildings
7. Government aid still only a hope. Some aid in a few states
8. Many lay principals; increasing annually
9. 80-85% lay faculty
10. Religious travel to schools; live elsewhere
11. Increasing percentage of non-Catholics
12. Need for public relations to encourage attendance
13. Ethnic diversity
14. Class size smaller—35 and lower
15. Departmental programs and variations thereof

16. Widely varying capabilities of learning
17. As high as one-third from single parent families
18. Two-thirds of the schools have kindergartens
19. Nursery schools developing
20. Policy—principal/laity/HSA/pastor
21. Much civic community activity
22. CCD, plus parish religious education program responsibility of Director of Religious Education
23. Most see themselves in relation to neighboring schools/parishes

FOOTNOTES

1. *The Catholic School* (1978) #78, National Conference of Bishops.
2. Vatican's *Declaration on Christian Formation.*
3. Higgins, Msgr. George, *Unionism in Catholic Schools Symposium Papers,* NCEA (1977).
4. Augenstein, John J. *A Collaborative Approach to Personnel Relations,* Washington, D.C. (NCEA 1980).
5. McBride, O.Praem, Father Alfred, *The Christian Formation of Catholic Educators,* Washington, D.C. (NCEA Monograph 1979).
6. *Ibid.*
7. *Ibid.*

SUGGESTED READINGS

Augenstein, John J. *A Collaborative Approach to Personnel Relations.* Washington, D.C.: CACE (NCEA 1980). A significant contribution to the process of collective bargaining, stressing and describing an alternative process with solid guidance and direction, the Collaborative Approach.

Kenserer, Frank, R. *Understanding Faculty Unions and Collective Bargaining.* Boston: NAIS, 1976. This is a Guide for Independent School Administrators published by the National Association of Independent Schools. A level-headed discussion of union issues with a valuable section in question and answer form and a useful glossary of labor terms and organizations. Stressed also are applicable personnel relations.

Fisher and Ury, *Getting to Yes, Negotiating Agreement Without Giving In.* New York, Penguin Books, 1983. Starts with "Like Life." Both authors teach and are members of Harvard Negotiation Project. The book is easily read, filled with practical anecdotes and examples of negotiating positions and problems and is loaded with practical advice and guidelines for any and all personnel negotiating situations. A very practical and easy to comprehend treatise.

McBride, Father Alfred, O.Praem., *The Christian Formation of Catholic Educators.* Washington, D.C. (NCEA Monograph, 1979). McBride develops the work of the "Christian Formation of Teachers Committee" (CACE 1979) in this monograph, detailing seven steps in the development of Catholic teachers; model programs of Christian formation.

Unionism in Catholic Schools, A Symposium. Washington, D.C. (NCEA 1976). Results of a three-day symposium on unionism in

Catholic schools, held at Bethesda, Maryland, at what now might be termed the height of union activity and problems in Catholic schools nationwide. Ten informative articles by administrators who were closely involved in various aspects of union activity. Presents theological, legal and organizational issues—all sensitive and important issues then and pertinent today.

CHAPTER III
JUST SALARIES AND BENEFITS

*by John J. Augenstein
and Mary O'Leary, O.S.U.*

Formerly Superintendent of Schools for the Diocese of Youngstown, John Augenstein has served Catholic education for over twenty years. He has made numerous presentations at NCEA meetings and is a recognized expert on Catholic school finance.

Sister Mary O'Leary is Director of Certified Personnel for the Diocese of Youngstown. She has worked extensively in the area of teacher compensation and directed the work of her diocesan salary committee.

CHURCH DOCUMENTS

Much has been written recently about the education profession and the perceived need for higher quality personnel. One of the factors receiving much attention is the need to make education a more attractive career so that schools may recruit and retain talented people. Higher salaries are only part of the solution. Many academically talented college graduates are choosing other professions which promise greater financial rewards, more opportunities for advancement and better working conditions. Beginning salaries for educators are frequently lower than those in other fields requiring a baccalaureate degree. Educators' salaries also reach a ceiling sooner and at a lower level than do salaries of other degreed professionals. Given this dilemma, the task of establishing salaries becomes complex.

Of the subjects addressed in this chapter "salary" (or wage) frequently receives the greatest attention in both the print and broadcast media when employee relations are the focus. However, there are other types of compensation, for example, benefits and leaves. The challenge for Catholic education is: within the spirit of church social teachings, there is a responsibility to provide appropriate compensation by blending employee personal and family needs with employer resources.

The church has spoken on the subject frequently. Nearly 100 years ago (1881), Pope Leo XIII in his encyclical, *Rerum Novarum*, addressed the issue of wages when he wrote: "To labor is to exert one's self for the sake of procuring what is necessary for the purposes of life, and most of all for self preservation."[1] and further on he noted:

"Let it be granted, then, that, as a rule, workman and employer should make free agreements, and in particular should freely agree as to wages; nevertheless, there is a dictate of nature more imperious and more ancient than any bargain between man and men, that the remuneration must be enough to support the wage-earner in reasonable and frugal comfort."[2]

Commemorating Pope Leo's encyclical in 1931, Pope Pius XI penned in *Quadragesimo Anno:* "In estimating a just wage, not one consideration alone but many must be taken into account."[3]

Thirty years later (1961) in *Mater et Magistra,* Pope John XXIII was even more detailed on the subject of wages:

" . . . in this matter (remuneration), the norms of justice and equity should be strictly observed. This requires that workers receive a wage sufficient to lead a life worthy of man and to fulfill family responsibilities properly. But in determining what constitutes an appropriate wage, the following must necessarily be taken into account—first of all, the contribution of individuals to the economic effort; the economic state of the enterprises within which they work, the requirements of each community as regards overall employment."[4]

And most recently (1981) Pope John Paul II, commemorating the 90th anniversary of *Rerum Novarum,* stated in *Laborem Exercens:*

"Just remuneration for the work of an adult who is responsible for a family means remunerating which will suffice for establishing and properly maintaining a family and for providing security for its future . . . Besides wages, various social benefits intended to ensure the life and health of workers and their families play a part . . . health care . . . holiday or vacation . . . pension and . . . insurance for old age and in case of accidents at work."[5]

The *National Catechetical Directory* sums up the church's social teaching when it states that "the fundamental concept underlying the social teaching of the Church is the dignity of the person . . . ."[6]

This chapter, then, will provide some information, recommendations, and examples of how compensation is being addressed in Catholic schools. The chapter has three principal parts which respond to these questions.

1. How can this challenge (blending of needs and resources) be ac-

complished? (process)

2. What are some forms of compensation and what elements are included? (types, elements, samples)
3. What does current survey research offer on the subject? (1984 Youngstown, Ohio Diocesan Survey)

PROCESS

Several years ago a study was conducted of more than 600 situations in which employees unionized. The study indicated five principal employer errors which contributed to unionization.

1. The employer gave the employees only minimal information about the status of the company's health—its financial position, its goals.
2. The employer introduced changes in equipment, schedule, and policy without advance notice or subsequent explanation to employees.
3. The employer made key decisions in a vacuum of ignorance about what employees wanted or needed.
4. The employer used pressure tactics, not leadership, to stimulate performance and cooperation.
5. The employer played down employee dissatisfaction.

The study is cited here not because employees unionized but rather to highlight some possibly frequent mistakes made by employers. Particularly important from that list for this chapter are numbers 1, 3 and 5.

The error list above illustrates the importance of involving all of the appropriate persons in decisions which affect them. Thus, compensation (salary, benefits, leaves, etc.) determination is not a unilateral decision. It, too, requires involvement of appropriate persons.

Those most directly affected by these monetary items are teachers, parents, parishioners, principal, pastor. Teachers have personal and family needs. Parents contribute support to the school through payment of tuition. The parish council, parish school board or parish finance committee, representing the large body of parishioners, usually has the responsibility for assisting or advising the pastor on the parish and/or school budget. The principal is usually the person who issues contracts and prepares the school budget. The pastor is the overall parish administrator, the person knowledgeable about the parish financial status. These people or their representatives need to be involved in remuneration discussions and decisions.

Those involved require some preparation and that preparation should include: an explanation of the purpose of the process, a review of members' responsibilities, the expectations of the members, and the time-frame within which the group is expected to work. (For additional suggestions, see *Procedure* section later in this chapter.)

There are both group and individual responsibilities. The overall responsibility of the group is to elicit the employees' needs and then to develop a compensation package which recognizes the differing needs and is within the available resources of the parents, school, and parish. The individual members are responsible for meeting preparation (study of materials), attendance, participation, and a willingness to arrive at a solution. Additionally, each member has a responsibility to keep the process from becoming an adversarial one. Thus, vocabulary and behavior are important elements in the process.

The process should be initiated by the pastor. The selection of participants should be done by each constituent group.

Information is a key ingredient for the group. Salary, benefits, and leaves provided in neighboring schools, dioceses, public schools district should be requested and shared. Such compensation packages sometimes provide alternate formats and options.

Employee needs have to be sought and shared. This is necessary because the remuneration package should recognize that needs of employees differ and thus choices should be developed and offered. To determine employee needs, informational questions need to be asked. Is more disposable income (salary) paramount? Are new or improved health care benefits more important? Is a retirement program provided or if one exists, does it need to be improved? Are there other benefits, for example, tuition assistance which should take precedence? What challenges are faced which require the establishment of specific types of leaves? It should be noted here that packages (choice options) may not discriminate against male or female, first and second income wage-earners, parishioners—non-parishioners.

Clear, accurate, concise (but complete) financial information regarding the school and parish (or diocese if such is appropriate) is another integral piece of information.

Finally, legal requirements such as social security (employer and employee shares), unemployment compensation, federal, state, and local taxes need to be identified and provided to the group. Social security information can be secured from the nearest local office. The remaining information can usually be sought from the diocesan fiscal office.

PROCEDURE

The next important question to be considered is how should anyone proceed to address the challenge. The following are suggested for important consideration.

1. This is a *group process* which will work to establish salaries, benefits, and leaves acceptable to all parties involved. It is not a unilateral responsibility of either pastor or principal. Thus, in-service should be provided in the areas of group dynamics, problem solving, conflict resolution, consensus decision-making and other organizational development tools which are deemed useful. Consensus decision-making is specifically suggested because, although it is more difficult to learn and achieve, it better fits the parish and school community of faith concept than "majority vote" which is "win-lose" and divisive. (Even some unions and employers are moving from the industrial, confrontational win-lose collective bargaining to a less or non-adversarial model generically known as "win-win.") The in-service programs may best be provided by the diocese through its own staff, if such expertise exists there, or contracting with an outside source, for example, a university management consulting firm. Another possibility is for schools or parishes in an area to contract collectively with an organizational service. Such service effort can provide quality service frequently not affordable by a single school or parish.

2. Using some of the frequently stated guides for group problem solving, the following are suggested steps.
   a. *Define the Subject*
      What is to be considered based upon expressed needs? salary? benefit(s)? leave(s)? (Consider one issue at a time and then blend the solutions at the end into a package for final consideration.)
   b. *Propose Alternative Solutions*
      What are the different ways to reach the solution? (List them.)
   c. *Analyze Alternative Solutions*
      For each solution ask:
      What resources are required? (people, time, money, materials)
      What are the benefits? What are the constraints? Can they be reduced? How?
   d. *Select Best Alternative Solution*
      On the basis of resources, benefits, constraints, etc., which solution best fits the needs and is achievable?
   e. *Plan Solution Implementation*

What action must be taken to implement the solution? Who is responsible for what? When must the action take place?

   f. *Implement the Solution*

   g. *Evaluate the Solution*

Was the solution agreed upon achieved? Was the plan for implementation followed? (Were there hindrances which must be resolved?)

3. Finally, although the process is primarily addressing the mundane but volatile subject of money, it is important to note that the process must mesh with the community of faith concept. Thus, prayer and reflection are an integral part of the process.

The process should be initiated early enough to allow for thorough consideration of issues and it should be completed in sufficient time for both the employer and employee to plan and budget for the next year in which the solution will be implemented. For example, if the process is initiated in September or October, it should be able to be completed by February or early March.

The group should meet as frequently as necessary to complete the process.

The process is not a panacea. There will be conflict and frustration because it requires the involvement of human beings and because it is addressing the controversial subject of money. However, if the participants approach the process with an attitude which affirms that a group solution is achievable and behave in a Christ-like manner, then the church's social teaching regarding labor can be implemented within the parish and school.

THE WAGE PACKAGE

Salary Plans

As noted in the chapter's introduction, this segment speaks to types of wage plans, possible fringe benefits and leaves. Salary and benefits together equal what is frequently termed "the wage package." Both require an investment of dollars by the employer. Often, however, employees fail to realize and/or acknowledge the equivalent dollar value of fringe benefits which is provided in addition to the basic salary or wage.

Subsections of this part will address legal requirements, two salary plans (indexed and merit), fringe benefits, stipends and benefits for religious and various types of leaves.

Legal Requirements

Legislative regulations must be observed in the development of a salary plan. Such federal laws as the Equal Pay Act, the Civil Rights Act, and the Fair Labor Standards Act will have an impact on how employees are paid. The diocesan finance office or local public accounting firms can provide information on these requirements.

Customary Elements of Indexed Salary Plan

The most frequently used salary plan is the indexed scale. Two factors that are most often built into indexed salary plans are years of service and education beyond the minimum requirement for certification.

An indexed scale is developed by determining a base salary amount and then establishing an index that provides a percentage of increase on the base for each year of experience and designated semester or quarter hours of credit beyond the Bachelor's degree.

Two sample indexed scales are shown in Appendix A. In Sample 1, a .045 index is used throughout, thus providing a uniform increment for each year of experience and for each credit category advancement. In Sample 2, two indices are used. The Bachelor's degree categories (BA and BA + 15) are computed on the .045 index and the Master's degree categories (MA and MA + 15 and MA + 30) are figured on a .05 index. Such a plan provides a larger increment for increased academic education.

Selected Elements of a Merit Pay Plan

Salary plans may be determined also by considering a teacher's past performance and the amount of responsibility accepted. This method is popularly referred to as merit pay. The hesitation to use this method is sometimes based on the fear that it is entirely subjective and that salaries are left solely to the whim of the administrator. While seemingly subjective, a significant degree of objectivity can be built into the process.

Areas of responsibility for teachers, for example, can include class size, variety of subjects taught, extracurricular projects, and added supervision or administrative responsibilities. A percentage of increase is assigned to each area of responsibility and that percentage is figured on a pre-determined base amount and then added to the base.

Evaluation of past performance also becomes more objective when based on the accomplishment of performance objectives. A few important, useful measurable objectives are determined and agreed upon by both employee and administrator prior to the beginning of the work year. Then, before determining salary for the next school year, the objectives are reviewed and evaluated by the employee and the administrator and the result of that evaluation becomes a factor in the salary determination, for example, how many of the performance objectives were successfully completed and what dollar or percentage increase will be provided for each completed objective?

Credit for further education and years of service can be incorporated into this method by assigning a percentage of increase to each designated number of semester or quarter hours of college credit and for each year or ranges of years of service. The percentage of increase is also to be computed on the base amount and added to the base.

The advantage of the merit pay concept is its flexibility in recognizing the responsibility and performance of the employee rather than just crediting years of service and added college credits. An example of a performance-based plan which can be used for administrators is shown in Appendix B.

Fringe Benefits

In addition to the actual salary, employees receive additional compensation in the form of fringe benefits. Although employees sometimes see take-home pay as their only compensation, employers invest substantial dollars each year in fringe benefits. Some common benefits which can be provided are:

1. Medical and Death Benefits
   a. Group medical plan
      1. Basic hospitalization
      2. Major medical
      3. Prescription drug
      4. Dental care
      5. Eye care
   b. Life insurance
   c. Pension
   d. Tuition benefits
   e. Federal or state chartered credit union benefits, such as hospitalization, life insurance, and retirement are usually provided through group plans. Through such plans, employers are able to provide increased benefits for employees at less cost than the employee could have purchased the same.

In determining which benefits to provide, the needs of the employees must be examined and considered. Employee requisites include both personal and family needs and may differ from person to person. For this reason, some employers offer flexible benefit programs. Flexible benefit programs provide employees with choices for their individual benefit packages. Usually, employees are more appreciative of their benefit packages if they are able to select those which best fit their personal and family needs.

An important aspect of any benefit program is communicating it to the beneficiaries. The time and effort that is spent communicating the benefit program can result in added employee satisfaction. General information about the details of the program can be explained in newsletters or bulletins. Individualized information should be supplied in a yearly benefit statement which summarizes exactly what is being provided by the employer in addition to the "take-home pay."

Stipends and Benefits for Religious

Compensation provided to members of religious communities is considered a stipend rather than a salary and is usually paid to the community, not to the individual priest, sister or brother. According to Webster's, a stipend is "a fixed sum of money typically modest in amount; a regular allowance paid to defray living expenses." Religious men and women belong to communities and are fundamentally dependent on those communities. The communities, therefore, assume the obligation of providing for the material needs of the members.

According to the 1983 data provided in the Compensation Survey conducted by the National Association of Treasurers of Religious Institutes, stipends for religious in the educational apostolate vary from $200 to $900 per month. In addition to the stipend, usual benefits include health insurance, retirement pension, housing, and transportation.[7]

The exact benefits provided to religious are sometimes determined by individual dioceses, parishes or schools. However, in other instances, benefits are established by the bishops and general superiors of an entire state. This agreement, then, becomes the norm for providing benefits to all religious who are ministering in the state. (Refer to Appendix C for sample State Agreement.)

Leaves

A leave is an absence from one's work assignment and may be with or without pay. Kinds of leaves and regulations pertaining to leaves must be spelled out in detail in personnel practices. Such issues as length of time, compensation and fringe benefits during leaves, retention of seniority, renewal of leaves and the right to return to service are those commonly addressed in leave practices. Some prevailing leaves are:
1. Sick leave

2. Short term leaves
   a. Funeral or critical illness
   b. Personal
   c. Emergency
   d. Professional
   e. Paternity
   f. Jury duty
3. Long term leaves
   a. Maternity/adoption
   b. Sabbatical
   c. Extended personal illness
   (Refer to Appendix D for more detailed examples of these leaves.)

Salary Survey Research

As part of a salary study undertaken by the Department of Education and the Board of Education of the Youngstown, Ohio Diocese, a national survey was conducted in June, 1984. Surveys were sent to all superintendents of the Catholic dioceses of the United States which numbered 168. Questions were asked about the following topics (refer to Appendix E for Survey Questionnaire):

A. Number of teachers
   1. Lay/religious
   2. Elementary/high school
B. Teacher salaries
   1. Method of establishing
   2. Average salary
   3. Comparison between elementary and high school
C. Unionization

Seventy-six percent (76%) of the dioceses responded.

Information gathered indicated that 78 percent of the teachers in Catholic schools throughout the country are lay teachers and that 67 percent of the teachers are teaching in elementary schools. Fifteen percent of the dioceses reported that teachers in some schools are unionized. The percentage of unionization is somewhat higher in the eastern part of the country and is higher among high school teachers than among elementary teachers.

Teacher salary scales are established either by the diocese for all teachers in the diocese or at the parish or high school level. However, 69 percent of elementary teachers' salaries are determined at the parish level and 72 percent of high school teachers' salaries are set by the individual high school.

Only 17 percent of the dioceses reported that teachers' salaries are the same for elementary and high school teachers.

The average elementary lay teacher beginning salary is $10,114 and the beginning salary range is $7,000—$13,257. The average high school lay teacher starting salary is $11,234 and the starting range is $7,000—$16,000.

Eighty-one percent of the dioceses indicated that elementary and high school teachers receive the same fringe benefits and 68 percent of the dioceses reported that benefits are determined by the diocese rather than by the parish or high school.

In summary, this research indicates that:

1. there are about four lay teachers for every religious in the Catholic schools in the United States;
2. usually, elementary lay teachers' salaries are somewhat lower than high school teachers' salaries;
3. the majority of teachers in the Catholic schools are not unionized.

Salary and benefits are not the only things that count for teachers in Catholic schools. They are, however, important to teachers and recognized as such by the church. The complex process of establishing salaries deserves all the consideration necessary for the just remuneration of all teachers.

Appendices

A—Sample 1   Salary Scale—Single Index
A—Sample 2   Salary Scale—Two Indices
B—Sample 1   Administrator Salary Criteria—Merit Pay Plan
B—Sample 2   Merit Pay Plan Sample
C—Religious Stipend and Benefits—Sample State Agreement
D—Sample Leave Practices
E—Salary Survey Questionnaire

SALARY SCALE
SINGLE INDEX

Step	Index	BA	Index	BA + 15	Index	MA
I	1.00	8,700	1.05	9,135	1.1	9,570
II	1.05	9,135	1.1	9,570	1.15	10,005
III	1.1	9,570	1.15	10,005	1.2	10,440
IV	1.15	10,005	1.2	10,440	1.25	10,875
V	1.2	10,440	1.25	10,875	1.3	11,310
VI	1.25	10,875	1.3	11,310	1.35	11,745
VII	1.3	11,310	1.35	11,745	1.4	12,180
VIII	1.35	11,745	1.4	12,180	1.45	12,615
IX	1.4	12,180	1.45	12,615	1.5	13,050
X	1.45	12,615	1.5	13,050	1.55	13,485
XI	1.5	13,050	1.55	13,485	1.6	13,920
XII	1.55	13,485	1.6	13,920	1.65	14,355
XIII	1.6	13,920	1.65	14,355	1.7	14,790
XIV	1.65	14,355	1.7	14,790	1.75	15,225
XV	1.7	14,790	1.75	15,225	1.8	15,600

SALARY SCALES
TWO INDICES

STEP	BA		BA+15		MA		MA+15		MA+30	
	Index	Salary	Index	Salary	Index	Salary	Index	Salary	Index	Salary
1	1.000	$12,745	1.045	$13,319	1.10	$14,020	1.15	$14,657	1.20	$15,294
2	1.045	13,319	1.090	13,892	1.15	14,657	1.20	15,294	1.25	15,931
3	1.090	13,892	1.135	14,466	1.20	15,294	1.25	15,931	1.30	16,569
4	1.135	14,466	1.180	15,039	1.25	15,931	1.30	16,569	1.35	17,206
5	1.180	15,039	1.225	15,613	1.30	16,569	1.35	17,206	1.40	17,843
6	1.225	15,613	1.270	16,186	1.35	17,206	1.40	17,843	1.45	18,480
7	1.270	16,186	1.315	16,760	1.40	17,843	1.45	18,480	1.50	19,118
8	1.315	16,760	1.360	17,333	1.45	18,480	1.50	19,118	1.55	19,755
9	1.360	17,333	1.405	17,907	1.50	19,118	1.55	19,755	1.60	20,392
10	1.405	17,907	1.450	18,480	1.55	19,755	1.60	20,392	1.65	21,029
11	1.450	18,480	1.495	19,054	1.60	20,392	1.65	21,029	1.70	21,667
12	1.495	19,054	1.540	19,627	1.65	21,019	1.70	21,667	1.75	22,304
13	1.540	19,627	1.585	20,201	1.70	21,667	1.75	22,304	1.80	22,941
14	1.585	20,201	1.630	20,774	1.75	22,304	1.80	22,941	1.85	23,578
15	1.630	20,774	1.675	21,348	1.80	22,941	1.85	23,578	1.90	24,216
18	1.675	21,348	1.720	21,921	1.85	23,578	1.90	24,216	1.95	24,853
21	1.720	21,921	1.765	22,495	1.90	24,216	1.95	24,853	2.00	25,490

ADMINISTRATOR SALARY CRITERIA
MERIT PAY PLAN

LEVELS:

Level 1: High school and elementary school assistant principals.

Level 2: High school and elementary school principals. Department of Education staff.

BASE

Level 1: $11,000

Level 2: $15,000

KNOWLEDGE

Includes degree, state and religious education certification, and total years experience.

A. Degree and Standard State Certification:

MA	Base Figure
MA+15	+5% of Base
MA+30	+10% of Base
MA+45	+15% of Base
PhD	+20% of Base

Religious Education Certification

Advanced Level B (Undergraduate)

Advanced Level C (Undergraduate)

Advanced Level D (Graduate)

Advanced Level E (Graduate)

B. Years of Experience:

1% of Base per year

RESPONSIBILITY:

School size and staff size

A. School Size:

0—200	2% of Base
201—400	4% of Base
401—600	6% of Base
601—800	8% of Base
801—1000	10% of Base
1001—1200	12% of Base
1201—1400	14% of Base
1401—1600	16% of Base

B. Staff Size:

0—10	2% of Base
11—20	4% of Base
21—30	6% of Base
31—40	8% of Base
41—50	10% of Base
51—60	12% of Base
61—70	14% of Base
71—80	16% of Base

PERFORMANCE:

Percentage of base will be determined on the achievement of measurable objectives established for the previous school year.

MERIT PAY PLAN SAMPLE

Mrs. Heidi Thompson is an elementary school principal who has a master's degree and fourteen years' experience. Mrs. Thompson is principal of a school with an enrollment of 250 students and has a staff of sixteen teachers.

NAME __Mrs. Heidi Thompson__

POSITION____Elementary Principal__

SCHOOL __St. Ann School__

1984—1985 SALARY
Level 2

I. **BASE** $15,000

II. **KNOWLEDGE**
Degree and Certification
Status (Religious Educa-
tion and State) $ 750 MA + 15—increment
                                               of 5% of base

Total Years of Experience $ 2,100 14 years' experience
                                               times 1% of
                                               base

III. **RESPONSIBILITY**
School Size: **250** $ 600 Refer to Appendix
                                               B-1

Staff Size: **16** $ 600 Refer to Appendix
                                               B-1

(Including Government
Programs)

IV. **PAST PERFORMANCE**
(Cumulative) $ 4,798 Amount carried over
                                               from 1983-84
                                               school year

V. **CURRENT
   PERFORMANCE** $ 1,350 Determined by
                                   Superinten-
                                   dent on base
                                   of achieve-
                                   ment of per-
                                   formance ob-
                                   jectives
                                   amount = a
                                   percentage of
                                   base

VI. **TOTAL** $25,198

VII. **CURRENT SALARY** $22,948 Salary figure for pre-
                                     vious year

VIII. **DIFFERENCE** $ 1,500 6.5%

SCHEDULE FOR WOMEN RELIGIOUS STIPENDS AND BENEFITS BEGINNING JULY 1, 1983 TO JUNE 30, 1986

A. Stipend

1   The ordinary stipend to the congregation for services, per Sister, is $700 per month, 1983-84; $750 per month, 1984-85; and $800 per month, 1985-86.

Sisters giving part-time service in a program receive a prorated stipend, depending upon the portion of time for which they are serving. For each Sister, a contract is to be drawn between the congregation and the parish/institution indicating conditions of service, e.g., months of service, vacation, etc. Local diocesan policies regarding sick leave, holidays, holydays, etc., are to be observed.

B. Hospitalization

The parish or institution paying the stipend for the Sister, whether she is serving full-time or part-time, is to pay the total cost of hospital and medical insurance, including major medical; and it should cover the twelve months of the year, unless earlier coverage is provided by a new employer. Hospitalization will be on a diocesan plan or an equivalent amount paid to a congregational plan.

When a Sister withdraws because of health reasons, she is to be covered for the entire twelve months. This would not apply if the congregation withdraws a Sister for another reason. The change of plans should be completed at the end of the month when the Sister is withdrawn by the congregation.

C. Retirement

The parish or institution pays the full retirement benefit for each full-time Sister to her congregation. Retirement benefits for those Sisters working part-time will be prorated. Full retirement benefits are: $800 per year, 1983-84; $850 per year, 1984-85; and $900 per year, 1985-86.

D. Living Quarters

The parish or institution is responsible for providing and maintaining completely furnished living quarters for the Sisters who share in its apostolate.

1. Parish or Institution with Convent

Ordinarily, the convent will be used for living quarters. If the religious chooses not to use the convent, the parish or institution has no responsibility to provide other housing with the following exceptions:

    a. Sisters in an intercommunity staffing situation not living in the parish convent will receive for living quarters per Sister per year: $900 in 1983-84; $1,000 in 1984-85; $1,100 in 1985-86.

    b. In the above agreement, no more than $900, $1,000, or $1,100 in the respective years may be charged for living quarters.

2. Parish or Institution without Convent

A living-quarters allowance per Sister per year will be paid by the parish or institution where the Sister is serving to the congregation as follows: $900 in 1983-84; $1,000 in 1984-85; and $1,100 in 1985-86.

3. Exceptions

Retired Sisters, or other Sisters not receiving stipends, living in a parish or institution convent will not be charged for living quarters unless additional expenses are entailed.

E. Transportation

The parish or institution is responsible for providing for the transportation needs of the Sisters sharing in its apostolate.

Sections 1 and 2 below represent options that can be exercised by mutual agreement between the pastor or administrator and the Religious Congregation. If other agreements have already been entered into on the part of the Congregation and parish/institution, a change must be mutually agreed upon. Otherwise the stipulations listed below apply:

1. The parish or institution provides the vehicle, gas, maintenance, insurance, etc., for the complete operation of the automobile. The car is available for a twelve-month period. For extended personal trips, e.g. vacation, the Congregation negotiates with the parish/institution.

    It is recommended that, if more than four Sisters serve parish or institution, a second car be provided.

2. If the Religious Congregation provides the vehicle, the parish or institution will pay an amount per year for replacement costs of the car to be equal to one-fifth the total purchase price of the car; in addition, it will pay the actual cost for operating the car. No cost per mile figures should be used since such figures generally include depreciation which has already been covered by the payment for replacement costs.

3. When Sisters use local public transportation, the parish or institution will reimburse the congregation for actual costs.

4. Other options for transportation are under study and may be offered for implementation during the course of this contract.

F. General

The Bishops will administer and interpret the above agreement. Religious Congregations who find it difficult or impossible to obtain the stipend and benefits listed may appeal to the Ordinary or his delegate for resolution.

Where an exceptional situation warrants a change from the provisions of this agreement, an alternate proposal must have the approval of the Religious Congregation, the parish or institution, and the Ordinary or his delegate. Such a request for an exception may come from the Religious Congregation or from the parish or institution.

Some Congregations may feel they do not need the amounts specified. If this is the case, the major superiors of the Congregation may choose to return part of the compensation as a cash gift to subsidize ministry at the given parish or institution, or elsewhere.

1. Sick Leaves

a. A teacher shall be permitted one-and-one half (1½) days of absence for personal illness without salary deduction for each month of employment (September-June) completed (15 days per year) and such days shall be limited to a cumulative total of 150 days.

b. When a teacher's sick leave account is depleted, a day's salary is deducted for each day's absence.

c. A teacher who has exhausted his/her sick leave, or a new teacher, may be advanced sick leave which could be earned during the remainder of the year. Unearned sick leave charged to a teacher will, at the end of the contract year, result in loss of pay for the days unearned.

2. Short Term Leaves

a. Leave for family death

1. A teacher shall be permitted a maximum of five days per year for absence due to critical illness or death of a member of the family (child, parent, grandparent, brother, sister, spouse or other relative living in the same household) without deduction from the unused portion of the teacher's sick leave account.

2. A teacher shall be entitled to one day funeral leave for the death of parents-in-law, brothers-in-law, sisters-in-law, aunts, uncles, nieces, nephews and grandchildren without deduction from the unused portion of the teacher's sick leave account.

3. If more than the allowed number of days are taken, those days will be deducted from the unused portion of the teacher's sick leave.

b. Personal Leave

1. A teacher may be absent for personal reasons without salary or sick leave deductions not more than one day in any one school year. If a teacher takes more than one day, he/she will receive a deduction from his/her salary (not sick leave) for each day over the allowed one day.

2. Except in cases of emergency, requests for personal leave shall be submitted, in writing, to the principal in advance of the anticipated absence at least 48 hours prior to planned personal leave. Personal leave days do not accrue from year-to-year.

c. Emergency Leave
  1. Teachers are permitted one day of emergency leave annually, subject to administrative approval. Webster defines "emergency" as an unforeseen happening or condition requiring prompt attention. The Board defines it as a condition or urgency so important that absence from school is required to resolve the contingency. Emergency leave shall be charged to the unused portion of the teacher's sick leave account. Emergency leave days do not accrue from year-to-year.
    Approved emergency leaves are for such purposes as:
    a. Attendance at the funeral of a close friend or distant relative.
    b. Attending to legal or business affairs which cannot be resolved except during the hours school is in session. This does not apply if request relates to a second job or an individually-owned business.
    c. Being with a husband, wife or child leaving for foreign military service on a school day or taking a child back to college.
    d. Weather conditions so bad as to make it impossible for a teacher to come to school.
d. Professional Leave
  1. With the approval of the principal, teachers shall be granted without salary deduction, not more than two days per year to visit another school or to attend local, district, state and national meetings or conferences of a professional nature. The parish will pay for the cost of a substitute but will not be responsible for any other financial obligation (fees, transportation, meals, etc.)
  2. Requests for such professional leave shall be made to the principal at least seven days before the anticipated absence unless it can be shown that late notification necessitates a waiver of this time requirement.
    A teacher shall submit written documentation to validate attendance at such visitations, conferences or meetings.
    Such professional leave days shall not be deducted from the teacher's accumulated sick leave days.
e. Paternity Leave
  1. A total of two days of paternity leave shall be granted to each male teacher for the following reasons:
    a. to take his wife to the hospital;
    b. to take his wife home from the hospital;

    c. to stay with his wife in the event of complications.
  2. Such days will be charged to the unused portion of the teacher's sick leave account.
 f. Jury Duty Leave
  1. The teacher is to receive, from the parish, the difference between his/her weekly pay and the amount received while on jury duty.
  2. A teacher will be expected to teach on days when the jury is not in session.
  3. No days are to be deducted from the teacher's sick leave account.

3. Long Term Leaves

 a. Maternity/Adoption Leave
  1. A teacher may request and shall be granted an unpaid pregnancy leave of absence on the conditions set forth below.
  2. A teacher shall notify the principal and the superintendent's office, in writing, of her intent to take a pregnancy leave of absence. The notice must contain all necessary information including the anticipated date of delivery. This notice must also be accompanied by a letter from the teacher's physician stating that she is physically capable of continuing to perform her duties and up to what date, in the opinion of the physician, she will remain capable of performing those duties.
  3. Upon receipt of the information, the superintendent's office shall confirm, in writing, the pregnancy leave of absence.
  4. The pregnancy leave shall extend to the child's first birthday but may, at the option of the teacher, be for a shorter period of time. The teacher shall notify the principal and the superintendent's office in writing, at least 30 calendar days prior to her date of return. Such notification shall be accompanied by a letter from her physician stating that, in his/her opinion, she is capable of resuming her teaching duties.
  5. When the requested date of return substantially interferes with the continuity of instruction, then the principal or superintendent's office may adjust those dates to a more suitable time.
     The teacher shall be notified, in writing, concerning any adjustment of said dates.
  6. If a teacher's maternity leave extends into the summer preceding the school year in which she expects to return,

she should write her letter of intent to return to her teaching position by April 10, so that no other teacher will be hired to take her place.

7. Sick leave may be paid to a teacher on pregnancy leave of absence only upon written certification by the teacher's attending physician of the teacher's disability by reason of pregnancy or pregnancy-related condition during the period of the pregnancy leave of absence specifying the exact number of days of such disability. However, such certification shall not be binding on the Board. The Board reserves the right to require a statement from the teacher's attending physician from time-to-time regarding the teacher's condition.

8. When the teacher returns, she will return to a position in the school, but not necessarily the one she left.

9. When the teacher is reinstated, she will advance to the next step of the pay scale if she has completed at least 120 days of the previous working year.

10. When a teacher is hired to replace a teacher on maternity leave this must be clearly stated on the contract signed by the replacement teacher indicating the name of the teacher being replaced. Accordingly, when the teacher being replaced returns to her position, the teacher hired as the replacement clearly understands that he/she no longer has a position.

b. Sabbatical Leave

1. A sabbatical leave of absence will be granted for one year and must be concurrent with the school year.

2. No more than two members of the total number of teachers in each county will be granted leave under this section at any one time.

3. The teacher shall present to the superintendent a plan outlining the purpose and goal of the sabbatical leave. Such a plan will have as its primary purpose professional growth and must constitute a full-time program as defined by the university of attendance and meet with the approval of the superintendent.

4. Remuneration to the teacher on a sabbatical leave shall be the difference between the replacement teacher's salary and the teacher's expected salary for one year of leave.

5. Intent to apply for sabbatical leave shall be submitted no later than April 1. Finalization of the leave must be completed by June 1.

6. At the conclusion of the leave, the teacher shall present evidence that the plan was pursued. He/she may be required to return to the school system for a period of at least one year. If, against the wishes of the parish, the teacher fails to return for one year of service, he/she shall be required to refund the money which was advanced. Other failure to substantially fulfill the program as approved by the superintendent shall be cause for refund of the money advanced by the parish.
7. A teacher returning from sabbatical leave shall be placed on the salary schedule without having lost an increment step. The time spent on sabbatical shall be considered a year of experience.
8. Teachers who are on sabbatical leave shall retain all insurance, pension and other benefits in conformity with the contract and benefit plan requirements, provided that the teacher pays all amounts (including contributions normally paid by the parish) as billed, necessary or required under any such insurance, pension or other benefit plan.

c. Extended Personal Illness Leave
1. A leave of absence of one year duration may be granted and is not renewable. A leave of absence may be granted only for reasons of health verified by a doctor's statement or for further academic preparation.
2. A leave of absence must be concurrent with the school year.
3. A teacher who is granted a leave of absence is paid no salary for his/her year of leave.
4. Upon return to the system, the teacher shall be placed on the salary step following the step which he/she was paid on his/her last contract.

Diocese of Youngstown
Department of Education
LAY TEACHER SALARY QUESTIONNAIRE

Diocese _____ State _____

DIRECTIONS: Please answer the following questions by checking the appropriate blank or by providing a brief narrative response.

1. How many teachers are in the diocese?

   Elementary   High School
   Religious _____   Religious _____

   Lay _____   Lay _____

2. Are the teachers of the diocese unionized?

   Elementary   High School
   Yes _____   Yes _____
   No _____   No _____

3. If the teachers are unionized, with whom does the union negotiate?

   Diocese _____

   Parish/High School _____

   Other _____

4. Do elementary and high school teachers have the same salary scales?

   Yes _____

   No _____

5. If elementary and high school teachers *do not* have the same salary scales, how does the discrepancy affect the relationship between the two groups?

   _____

   _____

   _____

6. If the elementary and high school teachers *do not* have the same salary scales do you plan to work toward a uniform scale in the near future?

   Yes _____

   No _____

7. Are salary scales established by the diocese or by individual

parish/high school?

Diocese _____

Parish/High School _____

8. Describe the method or process used to establish salary scales.

_____

_____

_____

9. If salary scales are established at the parish level, is there diocesan review or approval of the established scales?

Yes _____ By Whom?____

No _____

10. Do elementary and high school teachers receive the same fringe benefits?

Yes _____

No _____

11. Are benefit packages determined by the diocese or by the individual parish/high school?

Diocese _____

Parish/High School _____

12. Do parishes and/or high schools have high school/parish school boards?

Yes _____

No _____

13. What is the 1984-85 starting salary for a teacher with a Bachelor Degree and standard certification?

Elementary_____

High School _____

14. Do the teachers and pastors seem to be relatively happy (satisfied?) with the salary process being used in your diocese?

_____

_____

_____

I am interested in receiving the results of this salary study.

Yes _____

No _____

SUMMARY

1. The task of establishing salaries, which is one form of compensation, is complex. It is a blending of employee needs with employer resources. The church has addressed the subject many times from Pope Leo XIII's *Rerum Novarum* (1881) to Pope John Paul II's *Laborem Exercens* (1981).
2. A study of employee unionization indicates five principal employer errors—minimal information about company's health, introduction of change without notice or explanation, employer decisions about employee wants, employer pressure for cooperation, downplay of employee dissatisfaction.
3. A process which addresses compensation of educators requires involvement of those affected teachers, parents, parishioners, principal, pastor. These participants will require preparation and delineation of group as well as individual responsibilities.
4. Information is a key ingredient for the group. Such information should include compensation provided by other Catholic schools, dioceses, and public schools as well as employee needs, employer resources, and legal requirements.
5. The process is a group process and it is suggested that decisions be made by consensus rather than majority vote. Thus, in-service will need to be provided in group dynamics, problem solving, conflict resolution, consensus decision-making, etc.
6. Group problem solving guides are: define subject; propose alternative solutions, analyze alternative solutions; select best solution; plan solution implementation; implement solution; evaluate solution.
7. Prayer and reflection must be an integral part of process but may not be used to avoid responsibility.
8. Process should be initiated and completed in sufficient time to allow for planning and budgeting for the next year.
9. Process is not a panacea. Conflict and frustration will be experienced. Participants' attitude toward group process and solution is critical to success.
10. Wages plans include both salary and benefits and require dollar investment by employer.
11. Federal, state and local laws and regulations must be observed, e.g. Equal Pay Act, Civil Rights Act, Fair Labor Standards Act, etc.
12. Most frequently used salary plan is the indexed scale. Two common factors in such scale are years of service and education

beyond minimum required for certification.

13. Some elements of a merit pay plan are amount of responsibility, evaluation of past performance, in addition to credit for further education and years of service. Such plan affords flexibility.

14. Employers invest substantial dollars in fringe benefits such as group medical and death benefits, pension, tuition, credit union. Fringe benefits should be determined on the basis of employee needs. Fringe benefit plans must be communicated and explained to beneficiaries.

15. Compensation for members of Religious Communities include stipend and benefits, e.g., health insurance, retirement pension, housing and transportation. Exact benefits are determined in several ways, e.g., by individual dioceses, parishes or schools or by bishops and general superiors of an entire state.

16. A leave is an absence from one's work assignment and may be with or without pay. Typical leaves are sick leave, short-term leaves (funeral, emergency, professional, etc.), and long-term leaves (maternity, sabbatical, etc.).

17. A national survey regarding number of teachers, teacher salaries, and unionization was conducted in June, 1984 by the Diocese of Youngstown, Ohio, Department of Education. The survey indicated that: there are four lay teachers for every religious in Catholic schools; usually, elementary lay teachers' salaries were somewhat lower than high school teachers' salaries; majority of teachers in Catholic schools are not unionized.

FOOTNOTES

1. Pope Leo XIII. *Rerum Novarum.* Paulist Press, New York (1939), p. 27.

2. *Ibid.,* p.28.

3. Pope Pius XI. *Quadragesimo Anno.* Paulist Press, New York (1939), p. 19.

4. Pope John XXIII. *Mater et Magistra.* Paulist Press, New York, (1961), p. 29.

5. Pope John Paul II. *Laborem Exercens.* St. Paul editions, Boston, (1981) pp. 46-48

6. *National Catechetical Directory.* United States Catholic Conference, Washington, D.C. (1979), p. 96.

7. National Association of Treasurers of Religious Institutes Newsletter #11, (September, 1983), Silver Spring, Md.

For Additional Information on Process

Augenstein, John J., *A Collaborative Approach to Personnel Relations,* NCEA Publications, Washington, D.C., (1980)

SUGGESTED READINGS

American Society for Personnel Administration and The American Compensation Association, *Elements of Sound Base Pay Administration* (Berea, Oh. and Scottsdale, Ariz., 1981).

Augenstein, John J., *Collaborative Approach to Personnel Relations,* NCEA Publications, Washington, D.C., (1980).

Chambers, Jay G. *Patterns of Compensation of Public and Private School Teachers,* Institute for Research on Educational Finance and Governance, Stanford Univ., Stanford, Calif., (1984).

Detlefs, Dale R., *Guide to Social Security,* Social Security Administration, Baltimore, (1984).

Division of Computer Services and Statistical Reports, *Salary Study School Year 1983-84* (your) State Department of Education.

National Catechetical Directory. United States Catholic Conference, Washington, D.C. (1979).

National Association of Treasurers of Religious Institutes Newsletter #11, (September, 1983), Silver Spring, Md.

Pope John XXIII. *Mater et Magistra.* Paulist Press, New York (1961).

Pope John Paul II. *Laborem Exercens.* St. Paul Editions, Boston, (1981).

Pope Leo XIII. *Rerum Novarum.* Paulist Press, New York, (1939).

Pope Pius XI. *Quadragesimo Anno.* Paulist Press, New York (1983).

CHAPTER IV
NEW WINE IN NEW WINESKINS: CHALLENGE TO ADMINISTRATORS

by
Muriel Young, C.D.P.

With over 43 years of teaching and administration in Catholic schools, Sister Muriel is currently Educational Consultant for the Diocese of Pittsburgh.

CHALLENGE

"People do not pour new wine into old wineskins. If they do, the skins burst, the new wine spills out, and the skins are ruined. No, they pour new wine into new wineskins; in that way both are preserved."

Matthew 9:17

Catholic education must always be alert to the signs of the times. To be contemporary and futuristic without abandoning useful tradition is to keep an eye focused on the world and an ear attuned to God. Outdated forms of education and policies not informed by contemporary wisdom must be set aside by the Catholic educator. Holding on to old ways of doing things in a new age is not what the biblical adage recommends. It is a new age. Therefore, new and better policies and practices must be operative in the Catholic school system if the long tradition of faith is to be preserved by this generation of educators and students.

From the Second Vatican Council in 1965, which directs that "in the establishment and direction of Catholic schools, attention must be paid to contemporary needs",[1] to the latest directive in 1982 which calls for an awareness of change that affects every aspect of life,[2] the church brings to the attention of all its faithful the need for study and vision in answering the call to continue the long history of a teaching church.

The documents continually draw attention to the responsibility of teachers to be concrete examples of Christian living, to mirror for the educational community the commitment of one inspired by the gospel.[3] Teachers are expected to be certified, to be well prepared both in the professional and religious realms. They need to fulfill these obligations towards excellence in teaching by reflecting modern day findings.[4] In addition, an adequate formation in Christian living is an indispensable duty which requires administrators to offer such opportunities and requires teachers to respond.[5]

If teachers in Catholic schools are expected to integrate life experiences, culture and faith,[6] if they're to be examples of service, of faith community, and models of professional skills, then policies and practices must continually be evaluated, and changes properly made so that the new wineskins will securely contain their treasured content.

Many schools under the guidance of apostolic men and women constantly in touch with new developing theological, psychological, and pedagogical trends, continue to develop and serve the church in its vision of creating the new city of God. Teachers realize their ability in a graced vocation to respond to the duties and responsibilities of a new era where global concerns, issues of justice, and the cry for peace are no longer pious or spiritual reading, but a call to develop a social conscience in today's twenty-first century adults. The social conscience will stretch enough to hold the new wine securely.

The hope is that in all Catholic schools, administrators and teachers will feel the need for self-appraisal in such a way that the need for collaboration, intensification, risk taking, and a willingness to change will allow Catholic education to become the new wineskin which will preserve the new wine. It is hoped that some of the following information, practices, and models will help those who search for the city of God, to find it through a gracious, loving responsibility.

ORIENTATION OF NEW PERSONNEL

If done professionally and sensitively, orientation will contribute to a smooth and friendly entrance into the faith community. Orientation includes all types of help given to new teachers to help them adjust to their position more rapidly and more successfully.[7]

Three different types of orientation exist and all could be very valuable and supportive to the new Catholic educator. Sensitivity to teachers would assure that material presented in these orientations complement and not duplicate other material.

Diocesan Office Orientation

This is usually given by diocesan office personnel. Often the superintendent of schools and other school office personnel are introduced to the new teachers, and a short welcome and briefing are given on the unique role and distinctive character of Catholic schools. Special diocesan programs and policies are often explained.

An acceptable agenda for the process might be:
1. Welcome and invitation to join the Catholic school family
2. Introduction to diocesan school office personnel
3. Brief description of Catholic school uniqueness in the diocese
4. Explanation of Christian formation programs offered at the diocesan level
5. An overview of special programs required at the diocesan level, for example, continuous progress, education for justice, vision and values.

Initial Individual Orientation

Even though the diocesan school office may provide orientation days for new teachers relative to diocesan policy, the success of new teachers and their integration into the total school program depends upon the quality of the local administration's briefing. New teachers coming into the system vary greatly in preparation, experience, interest, and creativity.

In preparing for individual orientation after a teacher has been hired, the usual procedure is to estimate how much help the teacher should receive. How much academic preparation and experience has this professional had? Was the experience in public or Catholic schools? Is the person a graduate of a Catholic college?

The principal needs to get to know each new teacher and to meet special needs that may be observed or requested.

The following guidelines will help principals to acquaint new teachers with individual responsibilities.

1. **Curriculum**
   Manuals, textbooks, curriculum guidelines are discussed.

2. **Handbook**
   The teacher should receive the "Handbook of School Policies" in advance of the orientation meeting to clarify questions centered on the handbook. Personnel policies will be a great part of this handbook. Discussing them prior to the opening of school could eliminate many future problems.

3. **Co-Curricular**
   Special duties assigned to the teacher, such as responsibilities for safety patrol, student council, etc. should be explained.

4. **Job Expectations**
   Lesson planning supervision, classroom management.

5. Religious Expectations

Certification of religion teachers should be explained, liturgical practices, customs for prayer and sacramental opportunities clarified.

Staff Orientation

Orienting new teachers takes time. Planning and organization is necessary. After individual orientation, the new teachers should be introduced to one another and to other staff members. This first meeting is the heart of the orientation program. An informal gathering where a social atmosphere prevails will give the new teachers a feeling of being welcomed and accepted by the staff. It can help to set a conducive environment for the building of a faith community. After the informal gathering, the principal should talk about the distinctive character of a Catholic school, the specific philosophy of the school, the need to set goals collegially, and the curriculum. Some information should be given about the student body, the civic community, and special programs. A briefing should be given on the "Vision and Values" program of the NCEA or the values program being used. Lines of authority should be explained.

A brief overall view of the school should be given at this time. New teachers need this kind of exposure to feel comfortable. The following places should be pointed out:

Entrances and Exits (procedures for dismissal may be explained at this time)

Offices

Faculty rooms

Rest rooms

Cafeteria

Library

Gymnasium—Auditorium

Computer room

Curriculum materials room

Activities room

Learning center

Classrooms

Guidance room

Health room

Fire alarm boxes

The critical part of the orientation program should be supplying new teachers with information and the materials that will help them to be effective in the performance of their instructional duties.

Handbooks

The Handbooks (faculty, parents, students) are given to the new teachers prior to the initial orientation. However, at this time, areas of emphasis should be brought to the attention of the teachers.

Faculty Folder

A folder should be supplied containing schedules, bulletins of special significance, information to be supplied to substitute teachers, forms required by the office, for example, absentees, cafeteria count.

Materials

Supplies ordinarily used by teachers should be distributed: plan books, seating charts, attendance records, record books, sample report cards, correcting pencils, paper clips, rubber bands, scotch tape.

Time should be given during the orientation days for teachers to become acquainted with the curriculum materials and supplies, to organize for the first day of school, and to complete forms required by the office.

The following guidelines may be used by the principal at the orientation to insure success in providing information for effective performance by teachers during the school year:

1. Uniqueness of Catholic Schools
2. Philosophy of the School
3. Goals and Objectives
4. Lines of Authority
5. Expectations:
   Grading System
   Achievement Tests
   Lesson Planning
   Pupil Attendance Record
   Pupil Records
   Meetings
   Means of Communication
6. Forms
7. Teacher Aides
8. Transportation of Pupils
9. Cafeteria Procedures
10. Liturgies
11. Library
12. Schedules
13. Fire Drill
14. Evaluation and Supervision of Teachers

15. Instructional Equipment
16. Government Programs
17. Parent-Teacher Association
18. Health Programs
19. Extra-curricular Activities

Many principals arrange for a faculty liturgy and social following the faculty orientation. A welcome letter from the Board of Education may be given at the social. The pastor should also be invited.

Extended Orientation

The following guidelines may be used by principals to extend the orientation of new teachers over a period of one to three years. Help may be given in these areas by the principal, educational consultants and other supervisory personnel.

Expectancies
Spiritual Growth of Teachers
Grading System
Achievement Tests—Administration of and Analysis
Lesson Planning
Record keeping
Homework
Preparation and Participation in Liturgy
Teacher Aides
Policy of Evaluation and Supervision of Teachers
Provision for Individual Differences
Parent-teacher Conferences Discipline
Extra-curricular Activities
Strategies for Teaching
Evaluation of Student's Work
Adult Modelship
Use of Computers
Class Management
In-Service Programs
Staff Development Programs
Self Evaluation
Inter-Intra Visitation

COMPETENCIES

In the long history of Catholic schools in this country, teachers have been called upon to be well prepared for the task of teaching. The church has consistently called for competent teachers in both the professional and spiritual aspects of the teaching vocation.

The *Declaration on Christian Education* indicates the great need for special training in both secular and religious knowledge. It expresses a concern that teachers be appropriately certified and well equipped to perform their tasks in a way that is contemporary, and then asserts that teachers must give witness not only by their teachings but by their lives.[8] Competency, therefore, is expected of teachers in their preparation and in their performance as professionals and as Christian models in the school community.

Because of the uniqueness of the Catholic school, there is great concern about the spiritual formation of teachers. It is the teacher who imparts the distinctive character to Catholic schools. Curriculum, environment, administration, activities of all kinds, are areas where Catholic philosophy must penetrate. But, unless teachers communicate a "Christian vision of the world and of education"[9] the school will not be Catholic.

The church allows the teacher to sip of a new wine when it focuses attention on the "vocation" of the teacher rather than a mere profession. The competency of a teacher reaches beyond book knowledge, extending to a call to a legitimate defense of personal rights joined to detachment, generosity, and a life of personal commitment.[10]

Every lay educator, then, should "become fully aware of the importance, the richness, and the responsibility to all of its demands, secure in the knowledge that their response is vital for the construction and ongoing renewal of the earthly city, and for the evangelization of the world."[11]

Consequently, while the usual categories in defining competencies deal with such topics as classroom instruction, professional preparation, etc. at this time in the history of the Catholic school, it is important to reflect upon the imperatives of the church in relation to the duties of those responsible for Catholic education.

An example of this reflection can be found in the Diocese of Pittsburgh. Here, the Federation of Pittsburgh Diocesan Secondary Teachers in their agreement with the Diocesan School Board are responsible to uphold the implementation of church directives. The agreement states:

> Whereas the Federation recognizes the sole right and duty of the Ordinary of the Diocese, functioning through the Board, to see that the schools are operated in accordance with the philosophy of Catholic education, the doctrines, the teachings, the laws and norms of the Catholic church are the sole prerogative of the Ordinary to determine what will be taught

and who will be permitted to teach in the area of faith and morals, the doctrines, the teachings, the laws and norms of the Catholic Church.

Whereas the Catholic school has a unique position in the catechetical ministry of the Church: "It is. . . widely recognized that Catholic schools are to be Communities of Faith in which the Christian message, the experience of community, worship, and social concern are integrated into the total experience of student, parents, and members of the faculty." *National Catechetical Directory*[12]

At the elementary level, the Bishop of Pittsburgh, Bishop Bevilacqua introduced the "Handbook of Personnel Policies and Practices" by stating that "the teacher in a Catholic school, no matter what the area of teaching competency might be, is required to be a model of Christian virtue for all students.[13]"

It is the duty of the pastor, parish boards, and principals to implement diocesan policy in regard to the competencies expected of teachers as called for in church documentation.

Teachers are to be Catholic and are to live in conformity with the faith and moral principles as taught and explained by the Magisterium. This policy is in no way intended to prejudice the employment of other religious denominations currently teaching in the schools. Where it may become necessary to seek exceptions from this policy, permission is to be obtained from the Catholic Schools Office.

As minimal professional requirements, all teachers must have diocesan accreditation issued by the Catholic Schools Office. Within six years a teacher must acquire advanced instructional certification from the State of Pennsylvania. The following is required to obtain diocesan accreditation:

1. Bachelor's Degree
2. State Certification
3. Twelve (12) credit hours of Catholic Philosophy and Theology or attendance and satisfactory completion of the prescribed course of study in Catholic Philosophy and Theology as offered by the Catholic Diocese of Pittsburgh.

Any teacher in the first year of employment in the Diocese shall have two years to acquire Diocesan accreditation.

All teachers of religion must conform with the certification requirements established by the Department of Religious Education of the Catholic Diocese of Pittsburgh.[14]

At the diocesan level and at the local level, administrators are assuming responsibility for the provision of programs in the Christian formation of teachers in Catholic schools. Retreat days or evenings of recollection, meditation, contemplative spirituality courses, spiritual renewal opportunities, and resource books for forming faith communities are all developing resources for fulfilling the goal of competent Catholic leadership in the teaching ministry.

The emphasis placed on the Christian formation of teachers in no way lessens the responsibility for excellence in education. The usual competencies expected of teachers continue to prevail and stress is put upon principals to provide excellence in the areas of classroom instruction, classroom organization, preparation and use of instructional materials, planning effective communication, consultation of individual students, professional participation, self-evaluation, and non-instructional tasks, for example, keeping attendance records, checking home assignments, etc.

When administration and teachers realize the need for collaboration to fulfill the goals of Catholic education; when each is aware that excellence is the result of spiritual vision as well as academic preparation and that teachers do better when respected rather than inspected, Catholic schools will be true to the meaning of the Christian message.

A model for expected competencies of teachers is presented in "Guidelines for Selected Personnel Practices in Catholic Schools," published by the NCEA.[15]

Supervision

Supervision as used in the context of this chapter refers to a "process of facilitating the professional growth of a teacher primarily by giving the teacher feedback about classroom interactions, and helping the teachers to make use of that feedback in order to make teaching more effective."[16] In defining supervision in these terms, Dr. Alan Glatthorn acknowledges that some important methods of facilitating professional growth are excluded, such as in-service programs and activities of teachers in the development of curriculum.[17] While these areas may be included in supervision, for the purpose of this article they are not.

Likewise, a distinction is being made here between supervision and evaluation. Often the two terms are used interchangeably. Since evaluation is not the same as supervision, although directly related, it will be treated separately in this article.

There is, indeed, a great deal of ambiguity, complexity, and lack of agreement in the area of supervision and evaluation among today's educational leaders. Regardless of the kind of supervisory conceptions adhered to, most seem to agree that the principal is the responsible agent for the process of supervision and evaluation. This responsibility may be an outgrowth of policy, tradition, or critical need.

Because most administrators are managerially or organizationally directed, the delicate task of working with teachers to improve instruction can be lost in the every-day pressure of managing a school. Often, then, the importance of instructional leadership yields to the perceived importance of more pragmatic details. One example is from a Tennessee study done by Lovell and Phelps (1976):

> More than 80 percent of the teachers surveyed reported that they had not been observed during the year in question, and when observations were made, they typically were neither preceded nor followed by a conference.[18]

Since the educational leader in the school, namely the principal, often falters in this all-important function, it is necessary that it be stated in the principal's job description. One diocese puts it this way: The principal directs, supervises, and improves all areas of curriculum by appraising teacher performance through:

1. Pre-conference for setting objectives
2. Informal class visits
3. Formal supervision at least three times per year
4. Post-conferences for evaluating objectives and submitting the annual Professional Report.[19]

Variations of supervisory paradigms abound. Therefore, diocesan office personnel and other administrative leaders need to analyze the variations in accord with the philosophy which shapes the beliefs and behaviors of administrators and teachers. Also, under consideration must be the number of faculty members, the number of beginning teachers, and the time alloted for supervisory activities.

Whatever form of supervision is used, it must always be in an interdependence mode; that is, decisions must be made collaboratively, emerging from responsible dialogue.

The purpose of all supervision is eventually to lead to better instruction. The beneficiary of supervision ultimately is the student.

Clinical supervision, introduced in the 1970's by Cogan and Goldhammer, is used extensively not only in the United States, but internationally.[20] It is important to note, however, that after twenty years, clinical supervision has become a conceptual framework from which alternative designs have been generated.

Glatthorn notes that, while clinical supervision is a complex process involving eight steps as defined by Cogan, it can be simplified to the following description:

It is an intensive process designed to improve instruction by conferring with the teacher on lesson planning, analyzing the observational data, and giving the teacher feedback about the observation.[21]

The following simplified forms are offered as an alternative model for principals and faculty members who choose to use a form of clinical supervision.[22]

EXAMPLE OF QUESTIONS ASKED PRE-OBSERVATION CONFERENCE

Teacher_____Observer_____

Subject_____Date_____
1. **Class Setting:**
    a. What have you and the students been doing the past several lessons?
    b. What is the topic of the lesson that will be observed?
    c. What is the physical setting of the class?
2. **Student Characteristics:**
    a. Are there any prerequisite skills or knowledge needed by the students in order to accomplish the objectives?
    b. Are there any unique characteristics of the students in the class?
3. **Objectives:**
    a. What are your objectives for this lesson?
    b. What will the learner be able to do after your instruction?
4. **Evaluation:**
    a. How will you know if the students have achieved the objectives of the lesson?
5. **Instructional Strategies and Materials:**
    a. What is your role in this lesson?
    b. How will the students be involved with you and with each other?
    c. What materials will you use in the lesson?
6. **Supervisory Role:**
    a. What should I focus on while observing your class?

PRE-OBSERVATION CONFERENCE

Teacher_____Observer_____

Subject_____ Date _____

1. Class Setting:

2. Student Characteristics:

3. Objectives:

4. Evaluation:

5. Instructional Strategies and Materials:

6. Supervisory Role:

POST-OBSERVATION CONFERENCE
SUMMARY

Teacher	Observation Date	Conference

Subject	Observer	Instrument Used

Lesson Reconstruction:

Commendations:

Recommendations:

Signature of Teacher	Signature of Observer

The signature of the teacher does not necessarily indicate agreement with the conference. The signature indicates that the conference was held and that the teacher received a copy of the summary and the instruments used.

Plains Local School, Canton, Ohio.

Other methods of supervision used more frequently in the past decade in addition to clinical supervision are summarized by Glatthorn in "A Workshop Packet for Catholic School Principals and Supervisors."[23] This packet of differentiated supervision gives an overview of the system including a rationale. In summary Glatthorn suggests the clinical mode for teachers new to the school, teachers having problems, beginning teachers, and teachers preferring this mode. It is then the role of the principal to provide this supervision or arrange for it to be provided. It is to be noted that while it is a timely and consuming process with its demand of intensive scrutiny, it is extremely rewarding to both supervisor and supervisee.

The second mode suggested is the cooperative professional development mode for teachers experienced and competent who like to work together. In this process, a small group of teachers work together for their own improvement, observing each other's classes and conferring about those observations. Teachers will ask the cooperating teacher to observe such areas as curriculum content, pupil behavior and learning, classroom climate and environment, and instructional techniques. In this endeavor, teachers overcome some of the loneliness of the teaching profession; it gives objective feedback and new ideas. At the same time, it creates a professional climate and dialogue among teachers. When this kind of supervision becomes policy in a school, the principal organizes the procedure initially, and occasionally monitors it to be sure it is progressing adequately. Precious time, then, is allowed for the more critical task of working with teachers in need.

The self-directed development mode is also used by experienced and competent teachers who prefer to work together. In this strategy, teachers systematically plan for personal professional growth and conscientiously carry out the plan over the course of a year. The principal serves mostly as a resource person for those experienced and competent teachers who are skilled in self-analysis and self-direction. The principal's role will be to help the teacher develop a plan for growth, helping the teacher find the resources needed, and eventually help the teacher assess progress.

In one diocese, a self-directed mode is used, emerging from a construct of diagnostic supervision. This professional growth plan is used by principals with support from educational consultants and with teachers collaborating with principals. It is directed towards a goal which the teachers hope to achieve during the school year. It is always concerned with some aspect of growth—personal, institutional, or professional.

The program reaps rewards when a written plan for self-directed development is discussed with the principal in a diagnostic conference.

The plan used in the Pittsburgh diocese and designed by Rev. Robert Duch, Assistant Superintendent for Secondary Schools and Director of Staff Development for the diocese, includes a series of tests: The Meyers Briggs Type Indicator to help teachers discover personality types; Learning Style Inventory for measuring strengths and weaknesses as a learner; and the Firo-B, which measures three fundamental dimensions of interpersonal relationships: "inclusion," "control," and "affection."

These tests form an important strategy in the plan for diagnostic supervision which is a part of staff development. They are important as an instrument because of the wholistic and humanistic approach which attends to the whole person and increases awareness of self. The personal inventories allow principals and teachers to experience themselves in relation to each other and the world about them. They are a valuable instrument in building an understanding between staff and administration for the growth of a faith community.

Networking, which is the third step in a five-step strategy plan, is used for informal exchange of information, ideas, and feelings among principals from separate schools using the process or among teachers in the same school. In this way, mutual support is provided and lines of communication are established.[24]

Five specific strategies are used to help principals assume a leadership for local staff development and organization development. Principals, in turn, will learn how to use the five strategies with their teachers. The five strategies are:

1. *Diagnostic Conferences* which are held between the educational consultant and the principal and then between the principal and each teacher. The conference focuses on professional, personal, and school needs initially determined through the completion of needs assessment surveys. "Professional Growth Plans" and "School Growth Plans," which are long-range action plans, are developed.
2. *Three Personal Inventories* which can provide information for the principal, teacher, and students:
   a. Important personality characteristics (Meyers-Briggs Type Indicator);
   b. Interpersonal behavior characteristics and compatibility with others (Firo-B, Schutz);
   c. Strengths and weaknesses as a learner (Learning Style Inventory, Kolb).
3. *Networking* which is the informal exchange of information, ideas and feelings among principals from separate schools who are preparing for a leadership role in staff development and organization development. Mutual support is provided. Lines of communication are established between principals and central office.
4. *Collaboration with the Staff* which is accomplished by the principal who conducts diagnostic conferences with the teachers, and who forms a long-range planning committee with the teachers.
5. *Formative Evaluation* which is the collection and analysis of data while the inservice program is in progress so that the analysis of data will lead to continuing monitoring of the program, and appropriate and timely modification.

CATHOLIC SCHOOLS OFFICE, Diocese of Pittsburgh

PRE-CONFERENCE PLANNING SURVEY FOR TEACHERS

PRINCIPAL _____   TEACHER _____

To the Teacher

Please select one area of professional needs, one area of personal needs, and one area of school needs that you would like to focus on in a diagnostic conference with your principal. The principal will take your suggestions into account when planning the conference.

PROFESSIONAL NEEDS	PERSONAL NEEDS	SCHOOL NEEDS
☐ Teaching Assignments	☐ Autonomy (the need to work relatively independent of close supervision)	☐ School Climate
☐ Curriculum Organization or Development	☐ Affiliation (the need to demonstrate mastery of selected concepts and skills)	☐ Student Motivation
☐ Instructional Strategies & Techniques	☐ Achievement (the need to demonstrate mastery of selected concepts and skills)	☐ Supervision of Teachers
☐ Planning for Instruction		☐ Continuous Progress
☐ Reporting to Administrators or Parents		☐ Basic Skills
		☐ Discipline
		☐ Gifted Program

CATHOLIC SCHOOLS OFFICE, Diocese of Pittsburgh

PRE-CONFERENCE PLANNING SURVEY FOR TEACHERS

(continued)

PROFESSIONAL NEEDS	PERSONAL NEEDS	SCHOOL NEEDS
☐ Non-teaching Duties in the School	☐ Approval (the need to be recognized for one's achievements, etc.)	☐ Learning Disabled Program
☐ Supervision of Extra-Curricular Activities		☐ Enrollment
☐ Participation in Staff Meetings	☐ Acceptance (the need for respect from superiors, peers, students, et al.)	☐ Finances
		☐ Drugs/Alcohol
☐ Evaluation of Student Learning	☐ Other (please specify) _____ _____ _____	☐ Other (please specify) _____ _____ _____
☐ Other (please specify)		

*Adapted from Frank Duffy's doctoral dissertation, University of Pittsburgh, Pennsylvania, 1979.

CATHOLIC SCHOOLS OFFICE, Diocese of Pittsburgh

PRE-CONFERENCE PLANNING SURVEY FOR PRINCIPALS

PRINCIPAL _____ DATE _____
DEANERY _____ SCHOOL _____ DIRECTORY NO. _____

To the Principal:

Please select one area of professional needs, one area of personal needs, and one area of school needs that you would like to focus on in a diagnostic conference. Your listed needs will be taken into account when plans are being made for the conference.

PROFESSIONAL NEEDS*	PERSONAL NEEDS**	SCHOOL NEEDS
☐Decision Making (the ability to facilitate efficient solutions to school problems)	☐Autonomy (the need to work relatively independent of close supervision)	☐School Climate
		☐Student Motivation
☐Use of Human Resources (the ability to motivate teachers and to give them an opportunity to do their best in school)	☐Affiliation (the need to belong to a group or to associate with others)	☐Supervision of Teachers
		☐Continuous Progress
	☐Achievement (the need to demonstrate mastery of selected skills and ideas)	☐Basic Skills
☐Religious Leadership (the ability to motivate teachers and to give them an opportunity to do their best in school)		☐Discipline
		☐Program Continuity

CATHOLIC SCHOOLS OFFICE, Diocese of Pittsburgh

PRE-CONFERENCE PLANNING SURVEY FOR PRINCIPALS

(continued)

PROFESSIONAL NEEDS*	PERSONAL NEEDS**	SCHOOL NEEDS
☐ School Maintenance (the ability to take care of schedules, assignments, availability of teaching materials, establishing systems for doing the work of the school, etc.)	☐ Approval (the need to be recognized for one's achievements, etc.)	☐ Gifted Program
		☐ Learning Disabled Program
	☐ Acceptance (the need for respect from supervisors, peers, teachers, students, et al.)	☐ Enrollment
☐ Communication (the ability to maintain effective systems of communication)		☐ Finances
	☐ Other (Please specify)	☐ Drugs/Alcohol
☐ Competence (the possession of necessary competencies)	_____	☐ Other (Please specify)
	_____	_____
☐ Leadership (the ability to provide a high level of educational leadership)	_____	_____
		_____

83

CATHOLIC SCHOOLS OFFICE, Diocese of Pittsburgh

PRE-CONFERENCE PLANNING SURVEY FOR PRINCIPALS

(continued)

PROFESSIONAL NEEDS*	PERSONAL NEEDS**	SCHOOL NEEDS
☐ Importance (the ability to make teachers and staff feel strongly that they are interesting persons in important positions) ☐ Liking (the ability to exhibit friendly feelings toward teachers and staff)		

(*)—Adapted from Will Schutz's "Leaders of Schools"
(**)—Adapted from Frank Duffy's Doctoral Dissertation, University of Pittsburgh, 1979

Catholic Schools Office, Diocese of Pittsburgh

DATE_____

PROFESSIONAL GROWTH PLAN

NAME_____ SCHOOL_____

Personality Type_____

Learning Style_____

Interpersonal Relationship Scores: Inclusion _____

Control _____

Affection _____

NAME:

PROBLEM:

OBJECTIVE:

STRATEGIES:

Time Line:
  The final mode of supervision as given by Glatthorn is that of administrative monitoring or informal observation with feedback to the teacher by the principal. Its value lies in the fact that it is a great morale builder, especially for experienced and competent teachers. It allows the principal to get an overview of the state of affairs in the school and at the same time gives high visibility to administration. It creates satisfaction among teachers and pupils in their quest for recognition.
  Information observations of this kind may later be a part of summative evaluation. If this is agreed upon by teachers and principal

collaboratively, it is recommended that anecdotal records be kept. These records should include date, time, and place of the observation with a brief description of the behavior observed. These records should be available for the teacher to examine. Both records of commendation and recommendation should be filed.

Informal observations should be a part of administrative monitoring. However, more experienced teachers who do not need clinical supervision, and prefer no alternative should become the beneficiary of this mode.

There is no doubt that supervision is the highest priority on the list of principal's duties and yet the least attended to.

Many surveys of teacher attitudes toward supervision have shown widespread dissatisfaction with both the quality and quantity of educational supervision. Teachers cannot teach themselves the skills of self-supervision, and would welcome diagnostic supervision, clinical supervision, or any other focus in supervision that combines intellectual rigor with sensitivity to the needs, interests, and abilities of all members of the school community. As educational supervision continues to mature in the 1970's there is an increasing recognition of the need for a high quality of supervision, and more educators are coming to see problems in the schools as problems in supervision, as well as problems in administration, instruction, curriculum, and counseling.[25]

In all forms of supervision, the personnel of Catholic schools, whether administrative or teaching, should keep in mind the uniqueness of Catholic schools, demonstrated by its call to community. This community has as its foundation the life of the Spirit and unites its members so intimately that Paul compares it to a body with Jesus Himself as the head. In this community all are concerned about the pain and the joy of other members.[26]

EVALUATION

Earlier in this chapter, it was stated that there is a distinction to be made between supervision and evaluation. The purpose of supervision is to improve instruction and ultimately benefit students. Evaluation is an appraisal of the teacher performance and is not primarily done for the purpose of helping teachers improve teaching skills or professional competencies, although this may be an outcome if agreed to by the evaluator and the teacher being evaluated.

At the outset, it is good to distinguish between summative and formative evaluation. Formative evaluation is teacher appraisal done for the purpose of helping teachers discover weaknesses, followed by suggestions to improve. Formative evaluation usually focuses on some area of teaching, as for example, questioning techniques, discipline in the classroom, or providing for individual differences, although it may focus on any area of professional growth.

Summative evaluation, the focus of this discussion, is one of the most critical areas of school management. It is critical because it can be destructive of teacher trust if not done with care, concern, compassion, and sensitive honesty. Since the object of summative evaluation is teacher competence and results in the use of objective data in making judgments about the termination of contracts, principals frequently procrastinate or even refrain from fulfilling this all important task.

Because of the function of teacher evaluation, it is necessary that guidelines be set up in a collaborative way between principal and teachers to insure honest, open dialogue. These guidelines should include:
1. Teacher's job description
2. Clarification of roles of principal and teachers in the evaluation process
3. Purpose and construction of evaluation form
4. Determination of the use of the results

A discussion on the above guidelines should be done early in the school year. Agreement on the criteria and development of the form should be done collaboratively. Some diocesan school offices provide criteria,[27] giving the principal and staff freedom to set up their criteria and form for evaluation.

An example of suggested criteria is:
1. Scholarship and professional competency
2. Professional ethics
3. Teaching personality
4. Classroom management
5. Cooperation with administration
6. Rapport with co-teachers
7. General estimate of effectiveness
8. Judgment
9. Willingness and ability to accept responsibility for general school program.[28]

Another example is:
1. Attention to individual needs
2. Lesson presentation

3. Pupil involvement
4. Use of educational media
5. Classroom management
6. Professional manner
7. General appearance of classroom[29]

These or similar criteria are used in most summative evaluations.
The limitations in setting up criteria is well defined by Pamela J.
Eckard and James H. McElhinney when they wrote:

> Educational evaluation is usually limited to the evaluation
> of teachers, ignores objectives, utilizes a simple design, obtains
> data from three processes, and is implemented by a building
> principal as one more year-end responsibility.
>
> The three sources of data usually include: (a) pupil's scores
> on standardized tests; (b) notes made following two or three
> classroom visits; (c) and completion of a judgmental checklist
> of behaviors not related to pupil outcomes.[30]

For these reasons it would seem that the necessity for collaboration between principal and teachers in setting up criteria is imperative. Teachers are more and more concerned, and rightly so, with the justice issue of input into the criteria and process for evaluation on which they will be judged.

It is suggested that an appraisal committee consisting of representative teachers from all levels be formed at the local level to finalize the general conclusions arrived at in the discussion between principal or administrative staff and teachers concerning both the criteria and forms to be initiated. It is significant for the whole appraisal process that it be a team endeavor.

Primary for an effective appraisal is the defining of roles. The teacher's job description must be clear, and the supervisor's role in the evaluation process be clarified. The procedure should be simple and uncomplicated and yet effective. In time, it will be necessary to make changes as need arises.

The teachers' greatest concern will be a clarification in general terms of expectation for satisfactory performance. Teachers need to know if the evaluation is based primarily on classroom observation—formal and/or informal; test results; supervision of all types; or a combination of all teacher-principal relationships.

A target date should be established for the completion of the task. Once the procedure is completed, it should be explained to the staff and implemented.

Diocesan offices, and administrators on all levels should be insistent that evaluation of teachers be done by trained personnel in supervisory practice; that evaluation be understood as a summation of good supervisory technique; that teaching-learning behaviors be documented; that reasonable help for improvement has been given by the principal during the post-conferences following observation. At the close of the session following the observation, the principal and teacher should document commitments made. It is the responsibility of the principal to give direction, and the responsibility of the teacher to put into effect the suggestions and recommendations made by the supervisor. It is assumed that the supervisor and evaluator are the same person, namely the principal.

The difficulty of appraising any teacher is intensified when there is suspicion that the appraisal will terminate the contract. Sound, honest, professional judgments require a superabundance of emotional maturity on the part of the evaluator. When adequate help has been given in good supervisory practice, and performance still remains below expectations, and when a reasonable time has elapsed between conferences, termination of service should be made in justice to the educational community as well as the teacher.

Many of the due process cases experienced in the past decade stem from the fact that teachers do not believe that principals have adequate information for decision making since they were never in the classroom for formal observation or never gave feedback after the visitation, or that teachers were unclear about the basis for evaluation.

The evaluation that is written on the accepted form at the end of the school year must be based on supervisory visits spaced throughout the year rather than a last-minute approach the week before forms are due in the superintendent's office or other administrative offices.

Evaluation and supervision, although differentiated in purpose, are related in process and should not be regarded as distinct activities.

When teacher and principal are in close contact during the school year, when each understands that responsibility resides in both appraisee and appraiser, when teachers invite principals for a supervisory visit instead of waiting for the principal to initiate the contact, and when principals realize that avoidance does not resolve problems nor improve instruction, the process of evaluation will tend to be more honest, just, and compassionate.

Written records of teacher performance may also be used as reference material for recommendations and for on-going improvement instruction. The experience of the year will allow both teacher and principal to look for a new focus for future action. Where weaknesses are indicated, the teacher may, with the help of the principal, set up objectives for improvement. These objectives or target settings may be a part of a professional growth plan the following year and, therefore, be futuristic in its appeal.

Another outcome of summative evaluation is the help it may provide for principals. After evaluating teachers, principals may critically evaluate self, by reflecting on their response to the duty of providing help for teachers. Often the lack of success of teachers may be traced in part to the lack of commitment on the part of the principals who must constantly focus on supervision as their most significant task. Some suggestions for approaching the appraisal conference with confidence, serenity, honesty and compassion are found in George B. Redfern.[31]

To avoid misunderstanding or lack of clarity in the matter of evaluation and teacher rating, each diocese or at least each school should present in the "Handbook of Practices and Policies" guidelines indicating a just, honorable, and Christian perspective. An example of such policy from the Diocese of Pittsburgh follows:

Teacher Observation and Ratings
7.1 All observations of teachers shall be conducted openly and with the full knowledge of the teacher being observed.
7.2 A copy of any observation report shall be given to the teacher observed within three (3) days of the observation.
7.3 If a teacher questions the observation report or disagrees with comments made, that teacher shall have the opportunity to present his/her reasons for disagreement with the observer.
7.4 Any observation report that is placed in the personnel files by the administrator shall be considered as an evaluation.
7.5 Any unsatisfactory evaluation must contain an explanation or anecdotal report.
7.6 A teacher must be notified in writing of any unsatisfactory evaluation.
7.7 A teacher who wishes to contest that teacher's rating must indicate to the evaluator his/her dissatisfaction or question within five (5) days of being informed of the evaluation. The teacher may request a conference with the evaluator.
7.8 If the rating remains unchanged after the conference, and if the teacher is still in disagreement, that teacher may file a grievance.
7.9 No rating shall become effective until all steps of the above procedure, if invoked, are exhausted.
7.10 Educational Consultants are to receive a copy of the professional

evaluation of each teacher by June 1.

OFFICE OF EDUCATION, DIOCESE OF LANSING
Plan for Evaluation of School Personnel
Policy Statement on Evaluation—DBS #4117

The performance of all instructional personnel shall be evaluated on a continuing basis. The evaluation shall be thorough, fair, and objective—an assessment of the teacher's total performance in the school environment. It shall be designed to assist teachers in the growth and development of professional abilities as well as to identify areas of strengths and weaknesses.

The building principal is the primary evaluator of teacher performance and shall be responsible for submitting a uniform evaluation report of the teacher to the superintendent and/or deputy superintendent.

Purpose of the Evaluation

1. To improve instruction.
2. To identify and reinforce teacher strengths as well as suggest appropriate measures for teacher growth.
3. To determine a teacher's ability to fulfill the Catholic philosophy of education.
4. To provide the superintendent's and/or deputy's office with a written report of the teacher's performance.
5. To make judgment concerning contract renewals.

Philosophy

Evaluation is a process whereby the effectiveness of the professional staff member is appraised in relation to predetermined goals and objectives, his own personal competencies, teaching conditions, and administrative procedures.

This evaluation shall recognize the worth of the individual and his unique role in fulfilling the objectives of Catholic education. The evaluation must serve to support and provide positive direction toward individual and group effectiveness.

Evaluation must serve to foster self-improvement and be a vital part of the total school plan to examine and improve the goals of Catholic education, the instructional process, and the educational process.

Criteria for Evaluation

1. Criteria for evaluation should be mutually understood by the evaluator and the evaluatee.
2. The evaluator and the evaluatee should be aware of two areas

of proficiency, namely, that which refers to potential and that which refers to already achieved competency as they relate to the established criteria.

Criteria for Evaluative Instrument Follow:

a. The evaluatee strives to fulfill the philosophy, objectives and functions of the Catholic school and consistently exhibits ability to give Christian witness.

b. The evaluatee displays competency in the subject area(s) and level(s) of instruction or areas of service to which he is assigned.

c. The evaluatee employs sound principles of learning and child growth and development.

d. The evaluatee makes effective use of instructional and/or professional methods and materials.

e. The evaluatee demonstrates competency in organization, management, and control in the classroom or area of service.

f. The evaluatee maintains written evidence of adequate planning.

g. The evaluatee evaluates students. He uses information gained to inform appropriate staff members, students, parents, supervisors regarding pupils' progress.

h. The evaluatee relates effectively to students, parents, and members of the staff.

i. The evaluatee interprets his professional practices and the resulting program to appropriate staff members, parents, and supervisors and uses this knowledge to assist in planning and improving the program of instruction.

j. The evaluatee maintains acceptable personal qualities.

k. The evaluatee is loyal to students, staff, community, and observes professional ethics in this relationship with students and community.

l. The evaluatee fulfills his extracurricular and non-instructional obligations in accordance with existing needs, regulations, and practices.

Procedures for Evaluation

1. The principal shall have the prime responsibility for evaluating the staff members directly responsible to him.

2. The faculty at the local level should be involved in the development of specific evaluation procedures (how criteria would be applied and measured, frequency of classroom observations, etc.). These procedures will provide the basic data for uniform evaluation report to be submitted to the Diocesan and Deputy's offices.

3. Prior to any official evaluation, preferably at the beginning of

the school year, a pre-appraisal conference should identify:
a) The nature of the teacher's total professional responsibility.
b) The establishment of performance improvement targets.
c) The nature of the appraisal process itself.
4. Projected target areas for improvement when determined by the evaluatee shall be summarized in writing.
5. All probationary teachers, those with less than 3 years of experience in diocesan schools and who do not hold Michigan Permanent Certification, shall be evaluated at least twice a year. These evaluations will be intensive, covering in detail the suggested criteria for evaluation. The first evaluation shall be made prior to December 1 and the second evaluation should be completed before March 31. During the second evaluation, the principal and the staff members will determine target areas for concentration during the next period of evaluation.
6. Every three years a written evaluation report shall be recorded for a career teacher, one with at least three years of teaching experience in diocesan schools and one who holds Michigan Permanent Certification. Additional major changes in assignment or changes in teacher effectiveness should be noted. The evaluator has the right to evaluate as often as he sees the need and may schedule intensive evaluations during the three year span. The evaluation shall be completed by March 31.
7. A conference should be held to discuss the evaluation. Both parties shall sign the formal evaluation report. The evaluatee's signature shall indicate he has read and is familiar with the evaluator's report but his signature does not necessarily imply agreement with the evaluation.
8. A copy of the evaluation report shall become a part of the evaluatee's personal folder.
9. When disagreement is present between the evaluator and the evaluatee, the evaluatee has the option of attaching his personal reaction in writing to the evaluator's report provided this is done within one week of the conference.
10. The evaluation report authorized by the Diocesan Evaluation Committee and approved by the superintendent and his staff will be used by principals in submitting reports to the Diocesan and Deputy Offices. These reports will be due by April 15.
11. The evaluation policies, procedures, and regulations will be reviewed periodically by a representative Diocesan Committee.

Also in the Diocese of Toledo there is a well developed process for Staff Growth and Development which includes information and forms on supervision, evaluation, and self-appraisal.

In the appraisal systems currently being used, there are weaknesses stemming from the fact that measurement problems arise when evaluating teacher performance in areas of Christian formation. Teachers are expected to be models of Christian living, they are expected to be experts in Christian formation of students, they are expected to teach doctrine, contribute to faith community and extend service, they are to integrate faith and living and culture. There are no specific criteria for measuring the unmeasurable. To try to do so would induce criticism of poor judgment, bias, prejudice, and subjective ratings.

It is suggested that principals or teachers looking for such help used "Teacher as Gift," referred to under "Job Descriptions," or the materials referred to from the Diocese of Toledo.

Job Descriptions

The records of the Common Council of Buffalo, New York for the year 1883 contain a thirteen-item statement outlining the duties of the "principal-teacher."[32] Through the years, however, job descriptions of school personnel have expanded. From the mid-nineteenth century through the twentieth, role expectancies have changed and developed as the school system itself became more and more complex. Today job specifications of Catholic school personnel must reflect not only the changes in educational and administrative thinking, but also the sense of mission as outlined in the church documents since 1965. The bishops bring to mind the need for newness in approach by stating:

"Rapid, radical changes in contemporary society demand well-planned continuing efforts to assimilate new data, new insights, new modes of acting."[33]

Therefore, in defining the duties of Catholic school personnel, it is necessary to approach them with new insights gleaned from the unique character of Catholic schools. The religious and spiritual values that were taken for granted in the pre-war and pre-Vatican years are now questioned in the pluralistic society of the 1980's. It is a difficult task in today's society to integrate faith and culture. Yet, "the integration of religious truth and values with the rest of life"[34] distinguish Catholic schools from all others.

The council said:

It (the school) aims to create for the school community an atmosphere enlivened by the gospel spirit of freedom and charity. It aims to help the adolescent in such a way that the development of his or her own personality will be matched by the growth of that new creation which he or she became by baptism.[35]

The task, then, is to identify for administrators and teachers the various dimensions of their role, not only as educator, but as Christian educator.

Job Description of Principals

In "Principal as Gift" Sister Gertrude Ann Sullivan suggests that it is important for principals to define the expectations they envision for themselves in the awesome task of administrative ministry. These include areas of accountability, administrative tasks, leadership behaviors, and professional skills—all accepted as the instrument to give freely to the Lord and his church the gift of self. In Sullivan's document, the description of what it means to be a principal in a Catholic school begins to take flesh.

It is assumed that to ensure the educational excellence of the school, the principal must have certain qualifications—academic preparation and certification as required by the State and/or the diocese: Christian leadership and successful teaching experience. The duties and responsibilities of the principal encompass all those activities and behaviors that assist those to whom they are committed in the specialized setting of the school in their search for intellectual, cultural, moral, and spiritual growth. The description of these responsibilities vary from diocese to diocese, and from school to school. However, there are certain fundamental guidelines basic to whatever form the job description might take.

As principals perform the various duties of the day, each might be categorized in one of three ways:
1. Administration
2. Supervision
3. Christian Leadership

As an administrator, the principal:
1. Recruits, evaluates, selects, and recommends to responsible authority, competent teaching personnel.
2. Develops with the staff a handbook of policies that delineate expectancies and gives appropriate information for smooth operation of teacher functions.
3. Ensures through appropriate communication that all school personnel, including government program professionals and paraprofessionals have an accurate description of responsibilities, and understand the Catholic philosophy at the heart of Catholic teaching.
4. Keeps records up to date; is prompt and accurate.

5. Prepares and submits required reports for the diocesan office, school board, educational councils or boards, etc.
6. Directs work of the secretary
7. Manages instructional materials by ordering, storing, and distributing. An inventory should be kept of all materials
8. Prepares schedules and school calendars
9. Schedules events and activities
10. Schedules and orients new teachers; plans faculty in-service and staff development programs
11. Distributes and interprets diocesan office communications
12. Assigns pupils to appropriate classes
13. Oversees pupil record procedure
14. Provides for special needs of pupils
15. Provides for special services, for example, library, transportation, health, cafeteria, counseling, special education
16. Inspects school plant and provides for janitorial service and attractive decor
17. Prepares annual budget with pastor and financial committee

As a supervisor, the principal:
1. Plans and presents orientation for new teachers
2. Assists teachers in professional growth through in-service, staff development, faculty meetings, conferences, inter- and intra-visitations
3. Encourages membership in professional organizations
4. Directs the testing program and studies pupil progress
5. Directs, supervises, and evaluates curriculum
6. Organizes and administers the school program
7. Interprets and implements philosophy of the school
8. Designates a responsible person as a replacement for the principal when absence is required and there is no vice-principal
9. Determines the duties of the vice-principal when applicable
10. Collaborates with pastor, school board, or educational council in decision making
11. Develops with teachers a faculty handbook, with parents a parent handbook, and with students a student handbook
12. Provides for and directs activities for parental involvement in providing a Christian education.

As a Christian leader in developing the unique character of the Catholic school, the principal:
1. Implements the three-fold purpose of the Catholic school to proclaim the message, to build community and to give service
2. Provides for liturgical experiences

3. Allows time for faculty prayer and reflection
4. Provides for Christian formation of teachers, and certification of catechists
5. Creates within the school a climate conducive to growth in spiritual and moral values
6. Cooperates with pastors to provide an atmosphere in accord with the pastoral, "To Teach As Jesus Did."
7. Provides for the achievement and maintenance of discipline with freedom
8. Presents an attitude of hopefulness in meeting everyday problems
9. Fosters an awareness of global issues
10. Practices the principles of justice in all decision-making, and provides for education for justice
11. Implements the Vision and Values program or similar program
12. Encourages social service projects
13. Implements approved catechetical texts

The principal, more than any other person in the school community, has a remarkable opportunity "to impart a distinctive character to Catholic schools."[37] As the primary leader, the principal assumes leadership for bringing the experience of Jesus into the lives of men, women, and children. As an instructional leader, it becomes the principal's privilege to promote the integration of gospel values with so-called secular subjects.

Descriptions of the principal's role from several dioceses follow:

ROLE DESCRIPTION (Archdiocese of Atlanta)
Title: Elementary School Principal
Qualifications: The qualifications of the Elementary School Principal in the Archdiocese of Atlanta shall meet the current standards established by the Southern Association of Colleges and Schools for the elementary school principal.
Responsibilities: The principal shall provide the leadership necessary in an elementary school to develop, maintain and support the implementation of the Christian philosophy and continuing growth of the students. The principal shall be aware that the administration of the school depends upon the cooperation among the administrators, teachers, pupils, and community. Together they work toward the goals set by the Atlanta Archdiocesan Office of Catholic Schools and the policies met by the Archdiocesan Board of Education. The principal is responsible for maintaining and improving the quality of the instructional program and for providing leadership,

direction, coordination and support for the staff that serves the school. The principal sees that the needs of each student are known and met. The principal is a leader in his/her community.

Specific Duties: To encourage a continuous evaluation of the total school program including personnel, equipment, supplies, and whatever the principal deems necessary to the program.

To develop with the Parish Board of Education the annual school budget.

To supervise, advise, and direct members of the faculty in their teaching programs and techniques and to work with them on an evaluation process to help improve their professional growth and effectiveness.

To schedule regular faculty meetings in order to establish and enforce all required rules and regulations, and to assure a well-planned, efficient, and effective school program.

To plan and establish all academic and personnel schedules with the faculty and to assure adherence to same.

To develop and/or maintain the necessary systems to insure that all official school reports and records are properly maintained and communicated to appropriate authorities.

To communicate regularly with the pastor and parents in order to keep them informed about the school and to listen to their suggestions and recommendations.

To attend the meetings of the Parish Board of Education, the Home/School Association, and the Parish Council in order to contribute to the coordination of the activities of these groups in promoting the personal, religious, and educational welfare of the students.

To review and exercise final authority over all school activities and programs.

To interview, hire, and terminate the services of school personnel after consultation with the pastor and the Parish Board of Education.

To make provision for adequate maintenance of plant facilities, secretarial services, teaching on a regular basis, bookkeeping services, and food service programs.

DEVELOPMENTAL GUIDELINES CONCERNING
THE ROLE OF THE PRINCIPAL
(Diocese of Pittsburgh)

I. The Principal organizes and administers the school program by:
   1. Scheduling students according to individual differences

2. Directing faculty subject assignments in schedule preparation
3. Appointing competent department heads
4. Observing local public school district *or* official diocesan calendar
5. Maintaining and properly categorizing student records
6. Using diocesan report cards effectively
7. Providing supervision for students at all times with at least one staff member
8. Supervising the use of Diocesan Curriculum Guidelines
9. Demonstrating adequate general knowledge of *Laws* pertaining to aid for non-public school students (cf. *Handbook #220*)
10. Evaluating effectively the special needs of students and seeking appropriate programs provided under the law.

II. The principal directs, supervises, evaluates, and improves all areas of curriculum by:
A. Demonstrating knowledge of curricular principals and implementation in the following aspects:
   1. the needs of the school population
   2. the nature of each subject
   3. the relation of the school curriculum to the general community which the school serves
B. Adhering to curriculum requirements and time allotments of the State and Diocese
C. Directing the choice, acquisition and use of textbooks and instructional materials by:
   1. using approved texts from diocesan lists
   2. supervising and evaluating consistency in the use of texts and materials according to the needs of students and the continuity of the program of studies
   3. overseeing purchasing procedures and inventory updating
D. Appraising teacher performance through:
   1. pre-conferences for setting objectives
   2. informal class visits
   3. formal supervision at least three times per year
   4. post-conferences for evaluating objectives and submitting Annual Professional Report
E. Using the approved and recommended testing program:
   1. standardized achievement
   2. I.Q.
   3. diagnostic

       4. basic reading series

       5. math level tests

       6. other

    F. Analyzing test results to improve individual student progress and school program

    G. Communicating test results to parents and local community

III. The principal interprets and implements the philosophy and objectives of Catholic education by:

       1. providing a written philosophy that is specific to the school

       2. providing opportunities for worship

       3. encouraging students to help each other

       4. soliciting auxiliary services of adults

       5. promoting student activities to help the needy

IV. The principal recruits, selects, and recommends for employment, to the pastor or his delegate, competent professional staff; provides the staff with effective leadership, and prepares a faculty portfolio to include:

       1. completed personal application form

       2. letters of recommendation

       3. copy of state certification

       4. college transcript

       5. transcript of additional credits

       6. diocesan accreditation

       7. copy of religion certification

       8. update sheet for religion certification

       9. recent contract

     10. teacher attendance record

     11. in-service attendance record

     12. health record as required by State (cf. Handbook –409)

     13. TA-10A form

     14. documented and countersigned professional evaluation of teacher performance and conferences

V. The principal establishes rapport with and among members of the staff and the student body by creating a climate for professional growth by:

       1. encouraging the spirit of Christian joy and responsible freedom through self-discipline

       2. supporting staff in growth toward a strong faith community

VI. The principal plans effective staff meetings and provides inservice education, adequate and effective instructional materials by:

       1. planning and conducting effective faculty meetings at least

once a month

    2. providing for participation in teacher in-service programs sponsored by the diocese, deanery, and other educational agencies

    3. informing the faculty through memos and/or newsletters

    4. attending meetings regularly as sponsored by the diocese, deanery, and parish

    5. providing orientation, direction, and evaluation of para-professionals

    6. providing professional materials for teacher development

VII. The principal establishes good community relations by:

    1. participating in community and civic affairs

    2. participation in parish affairs

    3. preparing parent newsletters

    4. providing for open house

    5. scheduling parent-teacher conferences (2)

    6. assuring teachers' attendance at PTG meetings

    7. discussing school matters and parish affairs with the pastor on a regular basis

    8. maintaining contacts with the local public school

    9. participating in parish educational plans

VII. The principal provides for health, library, and guidance services, and oversees maintenance of school facilities by:

    1. utilizing adequate health services provided by state and local agencies

    2. making the library readily available for student- teacher use

    3. making available adequate guidance services

    4. evaluating with the staff the effectiveness of health, library, and guidance services

    5. setting and implementing standards for cleanliness and good condition of the school with the maintenance staff, securing adequate heat, light, and ventilation in all areas of the school.

IX. The principal has responsibility for budgetary planning and implementation by:

    1. preparing the budget with the assistance of the staff, as needed

    2. submitting the budget to the pastor for approval

    3. operating the school within the limits set by the budget

X. The principal has responsibility to coordinate the efforts of all school personnel in their commitment to moral and spiritual values and to the achievement and maintenance of discipline

and excellence in educational programs, by:
1. developing and scheduling action plans based on the On-Going Evaluation for Conscious Growth
2. developing curricular concepts based on Catholic moral and cultural values
3. relating the curriculum to the basic religion course

XI. The principal guides the staff in developing a faculty handbook for the school and provides for its yearly revision by:
1. developing a process of preparing and/or updating the handbook
2. extending the faculty handbook principles into similar handbooks for parents and students
3. basing the provisions of these handbooks on the diocesan *Handbook*

COMPOSITE JOB DESCRIPTION
(Diocese of Lansing, Michigan)

TITLE: Assistant Principal

PURPOSE: To assist the principal in overall school administration by effectively performing assigned administrative responsibilities.

DUTIES:
1. Demonstrate a commitment to Christian education and to develop a community of faith within the school.
2. Work closely with the principal and perform duties assigned by him/her in an effective manner.
3. Function as liaison between principal and various assigned staff units, such as custodial staff, curriculum committee, counseling department, etc. In this capacity it is his/her responsibility to maintain regular communications with the assigned group and report issues of potential significance to the principal.
4. Provide overall school leadership and assume total responsibility for day-to-day operations in the event of the principal's absence.
5. Assist with review and monitoring of personnel, building regulations of federal, state, diocesan, and accrediting bodies.
6. Assist the principal in developing an annual operating budget for the school.
7. Maintain membership in professional organizations
8. Regularly attend seminars/courses and/or read professional directions, technology, and trends in education.
9. Maintain regular communications with staff members in staff meetings in order to foster an atmosphere of cordiality, to keep them informed and involved in school policy and program deci-

sions, and to acquire a better understanding of the staff members' strengths.

10. Function as the representative of the school at local events in the absence of the principal.

RELATIONSHIPS:
A. Works with: Total School Staff
B. Works for: Principal
C. Supervises: Personnel assigned by Principal

JOB DESCRIPTION
(Archdiocese of Atlanta)
POSITION TITLE: Assistant Principal
ROLE DESCRIPTION:

The Assistant Principal is the professional staff person in the school who assumes responsibility for the school in the absence of the principal. He/she should be a recognized educational leader whose qualifications closely approximate those of principal, and meet the requirements of Southern Association of Colleges and Schools. Current trends regard the Principal and Assistant Principal as a team with shared administrative functions. Although the Assistant Principal is often a full-time teacher, he/she is charged with some responsibility in such broad areas as curriculum, discipline, and extracurricular activities.

MAJOR RESPONSIBILITIES AND KEY DUTIES

Assume responsibility for the school in the absence of the Principal

Help with agenda for faculty meetings

Serve as liaison between faculty and Principal

Assist the Principal with Parish School Board and/or Home-School Association

Assistant Principal in preparation of reports

When deemed advisable, the Assistant Principal shall accompany and/or represent the Principal at the Principals' meeting or other educational meetings.

Participate in preliminary interviewing of prospective teachers.

JOB DESCRIPTION OF TEACHERS
In "Teacher As Gift," Sullivan describes the religious educator as:
1. Faith Facilitator
2. Instructional Leader
3. Life Learner
4. Team Member
5. Bridge Builder

6. People Person[38]

In this self-evaluation tool, a remarkable job description of the teacher emerges; one that describes not only the teacher but the Christian educational leader.

To be a faith facilitator, a teacher:

1. Brings the message of Jesus through instruction, but more importantly by the witness of Christian living
2. Integrates faith and culture, faith and life
3. Prepares and presents all instruction in accord with "To Teach As Jesus Did."
4. Integrates principles of social justice into all areas of the curriculum
5. Prays with the faculty faith community
6. Participates in and prepares with students for liturgical and prayer experiences
7. Uses opportunities for spiritual growth

To be an instructional leader, a teacher:

1. Understands and implements Catholic school philosophy,relating it to the learning-teaching experience.
2. Shows a knowledge of child psychology and the principles of learning
3. Provides for individual differences
4. Uses a variety of strategies for the purposes of the lesson
5. Demonstrates knowledge of subject matter
6. Makes daily lesson plans and long-range plans
7. Provides for pupil activity
8. Integrates pre-determined goals
9. Uses problem-solving techniques
10. Encourages self-directed learning
11. Organizes material
12. Gives clear concise directions
13. Maintains discipline with freedom

To be a life learner, the teacher:

1. Participates in staff development, in-service, inter-intra school visitation, and professional organization
2. Is an innovator or finds ways to collaborate with others

To be a team member, the teacher:

1. Volunteers help when needed
2. Finds ways to implement the service aspect of "To Teach As Jesus Did"
3. Cooperates with administration and staff
4. Appreciates and encourages giftedness in self and others

5. Support and trusts the diocesan school office and parish organizations

To be a bridge builder, the teacher:
1. Communicates with administration, parents, co- teachers, and students.
2. Helps pupils to work together cooperatively
3. Uses opportunities for peace making
4. Gives support to the weak and underprivileged
5. Demonstrates mercy and justice
6. Fosters group cohesiveness

To be a people-person, the teacher:
1. Loves and enjoys children
2. Shares in the pain and joy of families, administrators, and staff
3. Cooperates with home-school organizations and other parish organizations
4. Is available to members of the school community when needed
5. Provides opportunities for celebration of God's gifts
6. Participates joyfully in civic community affairs
7. Builds positive attitudes

In summary, it is primarily the witness and the behavior of teachers that give the distinctive character to Catholic schools. While they must be knowledgeable in subject matter, psychology and pedagogy, they must also demonstrate a practical knowledge of these sciences in the classroom. Because they freely commit themselves to the school by accepting a position there, they are obligated to respect its dynamic character under responsible leadership.[39] It is the concern of the church that teachers see their life style and character as important as their professional credentials.[40]

Handbooks may specify as the following example does general expectations of teachers:

The Diocesan Synod of Pittsburgh places upon the teacher the responsibility of exercising of "an authentic apostolate to the human and spiritual development and growth of students."

If the threefold purpose of Christian education is to be realized, it must be through their (teachers') commitment to give instruction to their students, to build community among them, and to serve them. Furthermore, teachers bring insights and experience to planning the total educational mission of the Church. We invite and urge their creative contribution to the effort of the entire community to meet the current challenges.

To Teach As Jesus Did.

The bishop of the Diocese of Pittsburgh is theologically and canonically responsible for the religious education of his people, children, youth, and adults. The bishop has delegated to the Diocesan School Board and the Director of Religious Education certain responsibilities in schools of the Diocese, and to other official persons responsibilities for establishing and maintaining Catholic schools. The authority of these agents is to be considered an extension of the authority of the bishop, and never in conflict with it.

Teachers bring more to their classrooms than their knowledge of a specific subject area. They convey by attitudes and by verbal and non-verbal communication their own value system. Therefore, it is important that every teacher accept the teachings of Jesus Christ and manifest this belief by a Christian way of life. It would be incongruous for an individual teacher to exhibit explicitly or implicitly an attitude opposed to the purpose for which the school exists.

A detailed outline of the teacher's responsibilities is published in the school's faculty handbook.

Although descriptions of teachers' jobs are generally given in handbooks, they are often too comprehensive to clarify specific duties. Descriptions of teachers' tasks need to be universal in the handbook, articulating general expectancies. A more detailed list of specific duties should be individualized. This will include:

1. Definite assignment of grade and homeroom
2. The number of students scheduled for homeroom and for each class
3. The scheduled time for cafeteria, bus, playground duty, etc., for which the teacher is responsible
4. The co-curricular activities to which the teacher is assigned

Although it is necessary from a professional stance to describe the work of educators, their job can never be a mere profession. It is distinctly a supernatural Christian vocation. The work performed in the setting of the Catholic school is sacred and calls for personnel commitment. Educators should respond to all the demands of this vocation and realize that which they do is vital to the build-up of the body of Christ.[41]

Personnel in Catholic schools is far more extensive than the position of the principal and teachers. Other personnel should also receive the articulation necessary to clarify their job description. These descriptions should be adequately explained at the time of hiring.

Job descriptions vary from person to person in the position. The following is a sample list of some dioceses having such job descriptions.

COORDINATOR FOR CHRISTIAN FORMATION
and
CONSULTANT FOR ELEMENTARY RELIGIOUS EDUCATION
(Diocese of Lansing, Michigan)

1. To develop and coordinate a program for the on-going Christian formation of teachers employed in the Catholic Schools of the Diocese of Lansing in the areas of spirituality and theology.
2. To oversee the requirements of certification for all catechists working in parish catechetical programs of the diocese.
3. Provide leadership and stimulus for the continuous evaluation and improvement of elementary catechetical programs and their personnel throughout the diocese.
4. Act as a resource person by offering a regular series of catechetical method courses and workshops.
5. Be responsible for the coordination of curriculum and programs of catechesis in Catholic elementary schools and parish programs.
6. Be a resource person for the latest programs, textbooks, ideas, and communications on elementary religious catechesis from the area, state, and national levels.
7. Represent the Department of Religious Education in matters of elementary religious catechesis at diocesan and regional meetings of directors/coordinators and serve as religion evaluator for diocesan schools' evaluation teams.
8. Represent the Department of Religious Education to national, regional, and local groups as determined by the Superintendent of Education.
9. Develop and maintain an elementary religious education resource center at the diocesan office.
10. Provide adequate publicity and communication with the public regarding the philosophy, programs, and progress of elementary religious programs in the dioceses.

COMPOSITE JOB DESCRIPTION

TITLE: Department Chairperson

PURPOSE: To guide the educational program of the department by administering course and textbook selection, teacher relations, scheduling, and budget, in accordance with total school curriculum and philosophy.

DUTIES:

1. Recommends teaching assignments and duties of those teachers in the department in accordance with master schedule while maintaining balance between departmental needs and equitable teaching assignments for teachers.
2. Supervises course selection and textbook selection for the department.
3. Prepares budgetary data based on his/her assessment of departmental equipment and supply needs and submits on a timely basis.
4. Places purchase orders for approved departmental materials and verifies receipt of ordered materials prior to submitting invoice for payment.
5. Monitors departmental purchases to ascertain they come within the approved budget.
6. Schedules and presides at regular department meetings in order to maintain communications with individual teachers, and to facilitate group interaction on various issues.
7. Functions as a resource person within the department and the school relative to the subject matter.
8. Maintains level of expertise on trends in education and subject matter through frequent participation in seminars, meetings, and courses, as well as regular readings of professional journals and communicates such information to teachers within the department.
9. Assists in the selection of teachers for the department by interviewing candidates and familiarizing them with the philosophy of the department.
10. Makes personal classroom visit to each teacher in the department at least once each semester. Shares written evaluation, based on the observation, with the teacher before submitting it to the principal
11. Assists in the decision to dismiss or retain a teacher in the department by meeting with the principal (and/or Review Board) and presenting his/her observations.
12. Collects, collates, and summarizes important statistical data on staff and students as requested by the administrator.
13. Functions as liaison person with local universities to assist in the placement of student teachers.
14. Coordinates the use of audio-visual equipment within the department.
15. Monitors departmental audio-visual equipment to determine that

it is in good working order, arranges for repairs as needed.

16. Supervises the writing and distribution of teacher guides, syllabi, and other instructional materials.
17. Assists new teacher in the department in his/her assignments and offers curriculum assistance when needed.
18. Regularly attends curriculum committee and department chairpersons' meetings and other meetings at which attendance of the department chairperson is required.

RELATIONSHIPS:
A. Works with: Other department chairpersons
B. Works for: Principal
C. Supervises: Department teachers and student teachers

COMPOSITE JOB DESCRIPTION

TITLE: School Secretary

PURPOSE: To provide clerical/recordkeeping assistance to the principal and/or assistant principal of a school, while maintaining confidentiality.

DUTIES:

1. Do typing as delegated by the principal and/or assistant principal.
2. Maintain personnel and student files in an organized and up-to-date manner.
3. Handle bookkeeping functions as directed by the principal.
4. Answer incoming telephone calls, screen and direct to proper authority.
5. Process school mail and route appropriately.
6. Assist the principal with contact to and assignment of substitute teachers.
7. Contact parents, according to school policy, to verify absence or tardiness, or in the event of student illness while at school.
8. Process student records and arrange for their transfer to or from other schools.
9. Orient, train, and supervise student office help or others who assist in main office.
10. Greet and direct visitors to the buildings.
11. Monitor use of the P.A. system and make authorized announcements in the absence of the principal.
12. Handle injuries and emergencies according to school policy.

RELATIONSHIPS:
A. Works with: Faculty, Custodial staff, students
B. Works for: Principal and/or assistant principal
C. Supervises: Student Assistants and other clerical staff members.

COMPOSITE JOB DESCRIPTION

TITLE: Athletic Director

PURPOSE: to function as master teacher for athletics; to supervise, coordinate, and facilitate the emotional, physical, and social growth of students by providing for them athletic instruction and programs that meet their needs; to assist coaches in developing and refining skills to instruct and guide the development of students.

DUTIES:

1. Recruit, interview, and recommend for hire the head coaches for the various school teams, pending the approval of the principal.
2. Evaluate the performance of all coaches and submit the evaluations to the principal prior to the next contract time.
3. Develop all inter-scholastic game schedules with the league director and the principal and distribute the approved and official schedule to all interested parties.
4. Determine the need for cancellation of an athletic event due to non-playable conditions, in accordance with league rules.
5. Arrange all assistance necessary for the smooth operation of all athletic events being held at the school to include: game help, guards, physical maintenance and preparation of surrounding.
6. Handle all travel arrangements for away games and meets.
7. Handle all ticket printing, sales, and collection for athletic events.
8. Supervise and arrange all athletic assemblies.
9. Make contact with visiting team well in advance of the contest, and provide necessary accommodations.
10. Prepare athletic budget for upcoming year and submit to principal. Monitor adherence to approved budget.
11. Prepare financial reports as necessary.
12. Oversee the release of any publicity data to news media.
13. Ensure compliance of all teams with regulations established by governing athletic organizations, Catholic League, Federal, State, and local ordinances.
14. Monitor eligibility of all athletes— particularly their grades and compliance with age/weight restrictions, if any.
15. Purchase required supplies as noted in budget.

RELATIONSHIPS:

A. Works with: League Officials (C.Y.O., etc.) and Parents Club or equivalent
B. Works for: Principal
C. Supervises: Coaching staff

COMPOSITE JOB DESCRIPTION

TITLE: Chief Custodian

PURPOSE: To maintain the physical school plant in a safe and functional condition.

DUTIES:

1. Keep heating system operating in a safe and efficient manner.
2. Handle minor electrical, carpentry, and plumbing repairs as needed.
3. Supervise or perform routine tasks necessary, on a regular basis, to maintain clean physical surroundings (sweeping, dusting, emptying trash, etc.).
4. Supervise and assist with snow removal, particularly in advance of the opening of school.
5. Be familiar with the correct operation and maintenance of any equipment used to perform assigned duties, and operate/maintain it accordingly.
6. Assist with the maintenance of grounds and external landscaping in an appropriate condition as needed.
7. Order necessary cleaning supplies on a timely basis.
8. Arrange subcontract work, when authorized, as needed.
9. Monitor physical plant conditions regularly to locate potential problems needing repair, and advise the proper authority.
10. Adjust schedule to allow flexibility for extra maintenance work of a special nature (e.g. evening conferences or open house).
11. Maintain up-to-date knowledge of building inspection requirements and serve as guide when inspectors tour the facilities.

RELATIONSHIPS:

A. Works with: School Staff and Parish Personnel
B. Works for: Principal
C. Supervises: Janitor, Subcontractors and Cleaning Assistants, if any

PERSONNEL FILES

The responsibility of personnel files is comparatively new for principals in Catholic school administration. Before the influx of lay teachers into the school, most religious communities filed the records of teacher certification, transcripts, etc. in the motherhouse community files. Principals had no need to be concerned about sick leave, absentees, or salary schedules and contracts. Even evaluation was the responsibility of the community supervisor. In little more than twenty years all this has changed. Today, the high percentage of lay teachers and diversity of faculty background make it imperative to keep an accurate record of all personnel information.

Common procedure for retaining data on teachers is to keep a file in the principal's office. This file remains strictly confidential. Only certain designated administrators as defined in a handbook of policies or documents of agreement have legitimate access to these files.

No other information may be given to any other person without a written authorization of the teacher.

Contents of File:

The personnel file contains all information pertinent to the teacher's personal and professional status. This will include:
1. Teacher personal data sheet
2. Transcript of credits
3. Certification
4. Religion and professional updating
5. Contract
6. Absentee record
7. Medical leave record
8. Information on insurance, retirement, and other benefits
9. Observations—date and appraisal
10. Summative evaluations
11. Anecdotal records—signed and dated
12. Letters of recommendation
13. Professional awards

Policies

Where the Diocesan office does not provide policies for the personnel file, school administration with the faculty should collaboratively agree on the rights of teachers and administration. In writing a policy statement, it is recommended that the following be included:
1. Procedure for the examination of file
2. Time allotted before the examination takes place
3. Kinds of information to be filed
4. Counter procedures on communication in file
5. Confidentiality
6. Handling of requests for information by others than those agreed upon.

The principal, as a good steward of the vineyard, aware of rights and responsibilities, will insist that all documents be submitted and filed. Every precaution must be taken to protect their privacy.

It is good practice to state this in the handbook policies on personnel files. An example follows:

ARTICLE 16

PERSONNEL FILES (Diocese of Pittsburgh)

16.1 If a school maintains a personnel file of teachers, the teacher shall have the right to examine his/or file upon giving a notice of one day to the principal.

16.2 No anonymous communications shall be placed in the personnel file of any teacher.

All other forms of communication must be presented and reviewed by the teacher. The teacher has the option to counter such presentations. The teacher has the right to obtain a dated copy of all materials in his/her personnel file.

16.3 The personnel file shall remain strictly confidential; only the teacher, the principal, and the superintendent, as agents of the Board, shall have access to the file.

    A. A teacher shall be notified of any request for information from the file.

    B. No information shall be made available to any person other than the aforementioned without the written authorization of the teacher.

STIPENDS FOR SERVICES

Catholic schools in their long tradition have been credited as institutions of Christian service. Lay teachers and administrators accepting positions in Catholic schools are well aware that their salaries are not commensurate with their public school counterparts. They readily acknowledge that contributed services are a vital part of their ministry. Attention is drawn by the bishops to the fact where teacher associations of one kind or another exist, they must always be mindful of the responsibilities which form the specific mission of the Catholic school, even as they are concerned for the rights of their members.[42]

Attending to personnel practices that are rooted in justice and based upon the community concept is basic to the mission of the Catholic school. Those responsible cannot acknowledge that action for justice is a constitutive dimension of the preaching of the gospel without addressing the concerns of personal and family needs of devoted teachers and administrators.

"Salaries are often inadequate, and supplementary employment is often a necessity. Such a situation is incompatible with professional development either because of the time required to work, or because of the fatigue that results."[43]

It is imperative that responsible leadership looks for resources necessary to provide the means to eliminate such practices. While salary scales have been somewhat adjusted, it would seem that a very real weakness exists in the area of reimbursement for extra service. Where some form of teacher association exists or where a few daring Spirit-filled responsible boards realize the need, an attempt has been made to give extra pay for extra work. Secondary schools lead in this attempt. Elementary schools are still struggling.

Policies such as the following show an honest endeavor:

EXTRA PAY FOR EXTRA WORK
(Diocese of Lansing, Michigan)
ATHLETICS AND OTHER 'AFTER SCHOOL' ACTIVITIES

In determining the supplemental salary schedule for those responsible for athletics and other "after school" activities, the following should be considered:
1. The Church's teaching on just wages
2. The person's experience, skills, and expertise
3. Administrative responsibility
4. Extra-time (after school)
5. Size of the program
6. Applicable state and federal laws.

Administrative Regulations *DBS FILE #4143*
Subject: **EXTRA PAY FOR EXTRA WORK**
ATHLETICS AND OTHER 'AFTER SCHOOL' ACTIVITIES

Employing institutions will determine "the supplemental salary schedule" for use within that institution, and the degree of an employee's administrative responsibility in light of his/her co-curricular job description.

Criteria for determining the supplemental salary schedule, and the schedule itself, shall be made available to employees, become administrative regulations of the local Area Board/Education Commission, and a copy placed on file with the Office of Catholic Education, Diocese of Lansing.

I. **Other 'After School' Activities::**

Forensics, Debate, Band, Glee-Club/Choral, Journalism, Year Book, Cheerleading, Dramatics, Retreats and Christian Service, etc. shall be determined by administration within a range between...2%-3% (ea.)

To figure Percentage Allowance:

A. Select Scale A, B, C, D, E, or F in accordance with the education and certification of the teacher.

114

B. Place the teacher at the appropriate step on that scale which his/her years of experience in the particular activity would entitle him/her. (For example: John Doe possesses a BA + 18, is in his 5th year of teaching and has completed 1 year as Band Director. His band directing allowance shall be based upon 2%–3% of the 3rd step of Scale B.)

II. **Athletics:**

To figure Percentage Allowance:

A. Select Scale A, B, C, D, E, or F in accordance with the education and certification of the teacher.

B. Place the teacher at the appropriate step on that scale to which his/her years of experience in the particular activity would entitle him/her. (For example: John Doe possesses a BA + 18, is in his 5th year of teaching and has completed 2 years as varsity football coach. His coaching allowance shall be based upon 10% of the 3rd step of Scale B.)

C. Extra compensation for assignment to athletic administrative and/or coaching duties shall be limited to not more than 20% of the teacher's base salary.

HIGH SCHOOL

—Athletic Director

Class A	14%
Class B	10%
Class C	8%
Class D	6%

—Coaching

1) Head Coach Varsity Football, Varsity Basketball — 10% (ea.)

2) Head Coach Varsity Baseball, Varsity Track, Assistant Coach Varsity Football, Varsity Basketball, Head Coach Junior-Varsity Football, J.V. Basketball. Freshman Football or Freshman Basketball — 6% (ea.)

3) Head Coach Golf, Tennis, Cross Country, J.V. Baseball, J.V. Track, or Assistant Coach Track, Baseball, J.V. Football, Freshman Football or Freshman Basketball — 4% (ea.)

ELEMENTARY SCHOOL
—Junior High Football or Basketball   6% (ea.)
—Baseball   4% (ea.)

EXTRA PAY FOR EXTRA WORK
(Diocese of Pittsburgh)

20.5 It is agreed that compensation for activities extending beyond three (3) hours per week, including athletics, shall be negotiated between the principal and moderator/coach. The Parish and Federation agree to the following guidelines for negotiation of compensation between principals and moderators of school activities.

   A. Wages shall be negotiated with consideration given to degree of responsibility, after school time and the number of students involved in the activity.
   B. The Activity Moderator must be reimbursed for all personal expenses which are associated with the activity, e.g., use of car from school to activity if needed (20 cents per mile), meals, and accepted extraneous expenses.

EXTRA PAY FOR EXTRA WORK
(Secondary Schools)

18.6 Department Chairpersons

   If the principal chooses to appoint Department Chairpersons (including guidance counselors and librarians), they shall receive compensation over and above compensation called for in Appendix B, C, for a full school year's employment as a Department Chairperson according to the following schedule.
   A. Departments containing 1 professional employee, $100
   B. Departments containing 2 professional employees, $300
   C. Departments containing 3 professional employees, $500
   D. Departments containing 4 or more professional employees, $600

   Department Chairpersons serving less than a full school year should be paid pro rata according to the above mentioned schedule.

18.7 Activities Moderator

   The Board and the Federation agree that compensation for the Moderators of the following activities will be set at the following minimum schedule.
   A. Drama $250
   B. Yearbook $250

C. Forensics $250

D. Newspaper $250

E. Student Council $250

F. Cheerleaders $250

It is also agreed that compensation for other activities, including athletics, shall be negotiated between the principal and moderator/coach. The Board and Federation agree to the following guidelines for negotiation of compensation between principals and moderators of school activities:

A. Wages shall be negotiated with consideration given to degree of responsibility, after school time and the number of students involved in the activity.

B. The Activity Moderator must be reimbursed for all personal expenses which are associated with the activity, e.g., use of car from school to activity if needed (20 cents per mile), meals, and accepted extraneous expenses.

TRANSFERABILITY OF WORK EXPERIENCE/BENEFITS

In the past, very little attention has been given to specific policies on the transfer of work experience and benefits. Generally, principals, school board, or pastors have negotiated such concerns on an individual basis. Many teachers perceive unfair practices arising from the lack of policy in determining salary scale, benefits, and seniority. In school "A" credit or half credit may be given to teachers transferring from the public school system while in school "B" no credit is given to a teacher transferring from a school in the same diocesan structure. Even within the same school, teacher "A" may lose benefits because of sick leave, while teacher "B" retains benefits in the same situation.

The church fails in her kingly mission of looking after the temporal welfare of her workers when the principles of justice are violated.[44] Well intentioned, honest administrators often fail to realize their responsibility for providing structures for the study of temporalities when setting up personnel policies. It is well to remember that justice is never based on intention, but rather on execution. When the bishops state that specific steps can and should be taken now by concerned parents, educators, pastors and others to ensure the continuance and improvement of Catholic schools,[45] it is presumed that the agenda for such improvement and continuity includes retention of qualified Christian teachers.

The following example in effect in the Diocese of Youngstown, Ohio, indicates carefully thought-out policy:

a. **Credit for Experience**

When an experienced teacher is hired, he/she should be given salary credit for up to five (5) years of teaching and/or administrative experience in other than Diocese of Youngstown schools and full credit for all Diocese of Youngstown teaching and/or administrative experience.

b. **Partial Years of Experience**

In assigning salary credit for partial years of teaching experience, 120 days of experience in a single school year should be considered as a full year.

SUMMARY

1. Catholic education must always be alert to the signs of the times. To be contemporary and futuristic without abandoning useful tradition is to keep an eye focused on the world, and an ear attuned to God. Duties and responsibilities for the Catholic education are a challenge that calls for new wine in new wineskins.
2. The church is clear in directives to administrators and teachers in fulfilling their duties and responsibilities. There is a strong emphasis on the formation of Catholic school personnel. All duties and responsibilities are seen in the light of "vocation" and a ready response to the call of the Lord.
3. Orientation is a necessary part of staff development that is ongoing. It creates a Christian and professional entrance into the school community. A specific agenda will ease tensions and be effective in providing guidelines.
4. Competencies are expected in all professions. In Catholic education emphasis on Christian Catholic adult modeling should characterize competency lists without excluding traditional professional expectations.
5. Good supervisory practice is the responsibility of principals. Policies for supervision need to be done in a collaborative way, involving both evaluator and evaluee. Procedures should be clearly identified. An atmosphere of sensitive awareness, justice, and compassion should prevail. The object of supervision is formative.
6. Evaluation is closely related to supervision and will be an appraisal of the behaviors observed during the supervisory function. Evaluations are the basis for contract decisions and, therefore, must be as free as possible from subjective judgment. Guidelines for evaluation must be incorporated into handbooks of practices and policies.
7. It is necessary that Catholic school personnel be acquainted with their role expectations. These should be defined and explained before signing contracts. Written job descriptions should affirm the uniqueness of the Catholic school educator and indicate expectancies of the document "To Teach as Jesus Did."
8. Personnel files should be kept as required by handbooks of policy. Due process, grievance procedure, affirmations, and recommendations, evaluations and certifications are all part of today's administrative agenda. Rights of individuals in all these areas of confidentiality are safeguarded by keeping such infor-

mation conscientiously in the personnel files. Policies on the rights of individuals to examine these files should be spelled out.

9. An area of deep concern is that of monetary reimbursement for extra work. While teachers are expected to give service as detailed in late church documents, they also have a right to live in dignity and to be rewarded for special services. Ways of providing stipends for such work must be studied and implemented.

10. Few explicit policies exist on transfer of jobs and benefits. Justice requires Catholic leadership to create ways of providing just and reasonable policy in a spirit of authentic dialogue.

All table wines lose their freshness and fruit and become unsavory and flat when kept too long in a cask. So, too, an unhappy condition prevails when policies and practices become unexamined standards over long periods of time. The good wine of duties and responsibilities with new and savory character, is preserved best in the wineskins of prudent change and caring communities.

FOOTNOTES

1. Walter B. Abbott (ed.), The Documents of Vatican II, "Declaration on Christian Education, " trans. Joseph Gallagher (New York: America Press, 1966), #9. p.647.

2. L.C.I.S., op. cit., #67.

3. L.C.I.S., op. cit., #52

4. L.C.I.S., op. cit., #78.

5. The Sacred Congregation for Catholic Education, *The Catholic School* (Washington, D.C.: The United States Catholic Conference, 1977), #78. (Hereinafter referred to as T.C.S.)

6. *Ibid.*, #37

7. Sister M. Jerome Corcoran, *The Catholic School Principal* (Milwaukee: The Bruce Publishing Co., 1961), pp. 253-54.

8. Declaration on Christian Education, op. cit., #8.

9. T.C.S., op. cit., #74.

10. L.C.I.S., op. cit., #37

11. *Ibid*

12. Federation of Pittsburgh Diocesan Teachers and the School Board of The Roman Catholic Diocese of Pittsburgh, Agreement between, September 1, 1983, pp. 2-3.

13. Diocese of Pittsburgh, *Handbook of Personnel Policies and Practices* (Pittsburgh, 1984), Letters to Pastors, Principals, and Teachers from Anthony J. Bevilacqua, Bishop of Pittsburgh (Mimeographed).

14. *Ibid.*, p. 1.

15. National Catholic Educational Association, *Guidelines for*

Selected Personnel Practices in Catholic Schools,, Secondary School Department and Department of Chief Administrators (Washington, D.C.: National Catholic Educational Association, 1975), pp. 6-7.

16. Alan A. Glatthorn, *Differentiated Supervision* (Alexandria: Association for Supervision and Curriculum Development, 1984), p. 2.

17. *Ibid.*

18. *Ibid.*

19. Diocese of Pittsburgh, *Handbook of School Policies and Practices* (Pittsburgh, 1977), #311.

20. Professor B. Gorman makes this observation and cites an example from the Project CLINSUP '80 from Deakin University, Victoria, Australia; see footnote #5 in "The Clinical Approach to Supervision," Supervision of Teaching, 1982 Yearbook of the Association for Supervision and Curriculum Development (Alexandria, Virginia), p. 35.

21. Glatthorn, op. cit., p. 7.

22. Forms used in the Plain Local Schools, 1982-83, Canton, Ohio, supplied by Gene E. Apple, Assistant Superintendent of Instruction (Mimeographed).

23. Alan A. Glatthorn, "Different Supervision for Catholic Schools," (A Workshop Packet for Catholic School Principals and Supervisors presented at the Supervision, Personnel and Curriculum Division of CACE, Orlando, Florida, November, 1982). (Mimeographed).

24. Forms referred to are from the "In-Service Program to Help Principals Become School Leaders of Staff Development and Organizational Development," designed by Father Duch, Ph.D., Diocese of Pittsburgh, 1981. (Mimeographed).

25. G. Bradley Seager, Jr. "An Introduction to Diagnostic Supervision," (University of Pittsburgh, 1974) (Mimeographed).

26. National Conference of Catholic Bishops, *To Teach as Jesus Did.* (Washington, D.C.: United States Catholic Conference, 1973), #22. (Hereafter referred to as T.T.A.J.D.).

27. Diocese of Pittsburgh, op. cit., #405.

28. Form used in the Diocese of Youngstown, 1982—11—11.

29. Form used in the Diocese of Pittsburgh. (Mimeographed).

30. Pamela J. Eckard and James H. McElhenney, "Teacher Evaluation and Educational Accountability," *Educational Leadership* (May, 1977), pp. 613-618.

31. George B. Redfern, *How to Appraise Teaching Performance* (Columbus: School Management Institute, 1968), pp. 87-88.

32. J. Cace Morrison, "The Principalship Develops Supervisory Status." Tenth Year Book, (Department of Elementary School Principals, N.E.A., 1931), p. 157, cited by Henry J. Otto and D. Sanders, *Elementary School Organization and Administration* (New York: Appleton-Century-Crofts, 1964), p. 348.

33. T.T.A.J.D., #43.

34. National Catholic Conference of Bishops, *Teach Them* (Washington, D.C.: United States Catholic Conference, May 6, 1976), p. 3.

35. Declaration on Christian Education, op. cit., #8.

36. Sister Gertrude Ann Sullivan and the San Diego Educational Team, *Principal As Gift,* 1979. (Mimeographed).

37. T.C.S., op. cit., #78.

38. Sister Gertrude Ann Sullivan and the San Diego Educational Team, *Teacher As Gift,* (Dubuque, Iowa: William C. Brown Co., 1979), p. 1.

39. T.C.S., op. cit., #80.

40. Teach Them, op. cit., 111, p.7.

41. L.C.I.S., op. cit. #37.

42. T.C.S., op. cit. #80.

43. L.C.I.S., op. cit. #27.

44. National Catechetical Directory, Sharing the Light of Faith, (Washington, D.C.: United States Catholic Conference, 1979), #30.

45. T.T.J.A.D., op. cit. #119.

SUGGESTED READINGS

Crow, Porter J. "Teaching and Motivating: The Jesus Model." *Momentum*, May, 1978, pp. 11-15. This article describes the attitude needed by teachers and administrators to deal with the critical questions arising from a changing future.

Glatthorn, Alan A. and Shields, Sister Carmel Regina. *Differentiated Supervision for Catholic Schools.* Washington, D.C.: National Catholic Educational Association, 1983. An important monograph to be used as a practical tool to enhance effective supervision in Catholic Schools. A resource guide for reported supervisory practices is included.

Goldhammer, Robert. *Clinical Supervision.* New York: Holt, Rinehart and Winston, 1969. An extensive presentation of the stages of clinical supervision, their rationale, and methods employed at each step.

Greely, Andrew M., McReady, W.C., and McCourt, K. *Catholic*

Schools in a Declining Church. Kansas City: Sheed and Ward, Inc., 1976. A study in value-oriented education and social change and their effect upon Catholic school education.

McBride, Rev. Alfred. *The Christian Formation of Catholic Education.* NCEA. Presentation of the seven tasks to be developed in forming Catholic educators.

McGreal, Thomas L. *Successful Teacher Evaluation.* Alexandria: Association for Supervision and Curriculum Development, 1983. The author portrays the process of evaluation as a constructive tool that should be carried out in an atmosphere of mutual confidence and freedom from suspicion.

O'Brien, Rev. Thomas T. The Catholic School Covenant. *Today's Catholic Teacher.* April, 1982, pp. 16-18. An explanation of the new concept of covenant as an alternative to unionization.

Redington, Patrick. "Justice for Teachers." *Momentum,* May, 1978, pp. 29-32. Practical ways to meet the needs of lay teachers in this new era of Catholic education is called for in this thought-provoking article.

Wojicki, Father Ted and Brother Kevin Convey. *Teachers, Catholic Schools and Faith Community: A Program of Spirituality.* LeJacq Publishing, 1982. A practical guide for directing dialogue between teachers and the church's vision for her schools based on the documents on Catholic school documents.

CHAPTER V
JUSTICE IN TEACHER TERMINATION

by
Mary Ann Corr, S.C. Ed.D.

Sister Mary Ann is Elementary Education Consultant in the Diocese of Greensburg, Pennsylvania. She has been instrumental in planning diocesan-wide teacher evaluation processes which she believes are essential to just personnel practices in schools.

Schools exist for the education of students. Thus, when a teacher continues to be ineffective after regular supervisory assistance and students are not being educated, there is a need to terminate the employment of that teacher.

In a broad sense, the process of termination for nontenured and tenured teachers has serious legal and ethical ramifications. While each state describes specific behaviors that are causes for dismissal, the most common reasons are immorality, neglect of duty, misconduct, incompetence, or other just causes, such as reduction in force. When reduction in force is a consideration, varied criteria should be used to formulate general procedures. However, other than reduction in force, where failure on the part of the teacher is in question, the school administration bears the burden of proving a "just cause" for dismissal.

CHURCH DOCUMENTS

Termination of employees in a Catholic school should generally follow the guidelines that are applicable for any school termination. However, the very purpose of the Catholic school and the role of the Catholic school teacher affects this process. Describing the purpose of the Catholic school, the Second Vatican Council in its Declaration on Christian Education states:

> By virtue of its very purpose, while it cultivates the intellect with unremitting attention, the school ripens the capacity for right judgement, provides an introduction into the cultural heritage won by past generations, promotes a sense of values and readies students for professional life.[1]

125

The role of the Catholic school teacher, while influenced by appropriate academic preparation, is characterized by a life-long commitment to the gospel message of Jesus Christ. In addressing teachers, the Council said:

They (teachers) should, therefore, be trained with particular care so that they may be enriched with both secular and religious knowledge, appropriately certified and may be equipped with an educational skill which reflects modern-day findings. Bound by charity to one another and their students, and penetrated by an apostolic spirit, let them give witness to Christ, the unique Teacher, by their lives as well as by their teaching.[2]

In accepting their position, teachers in a Catholic school pledge to respect and develop the uniqueness of each child they teach. The special task of the Catholic school teacher is to stress integration of every area of the curriculum. The American bishops in their pastoral message on Catholic education, *To Teach As Jesus Did*, state: "The integration of religious truths with the rest of life is brought about in the Catholic school. . .by the presence of teachers who express an integrated approach to learning and living in their private and professional lives."[3] The stress on integration, particularly as it applies to the influence of the teacher, is more clearly defined in a Vatican document, *The Catholic School.* It said:

The extent to which the Christian message is transmitted through education depends to a very great extent on the teachers. The integration of culture and faith is mediated by the other integration of faith and life in the person of the teacher. The nobility of the task to which teachers are called demands that, in imitation of Christ, the only Teacher, they reveal the Christian message not only by word but also by every gesture of their behavior.[4]

In addition to having expertise in one or more subject areas and being knowledgeable in human development, learning theory, and teaching practices, the Catholic school teacher has the opportunity to guide students spiritually. As the church has noted:

Since the educative mission of the Catholic school is so wide, the teacher is in an excellent position to guide the pupil to a deepening of his faith and to enrich and enlighten his human knowledge with the data of the faith. . . .The teacher can form the mind and heart of his pupils and guide them to develop a total commitment to Christ, with their whole personality enriched by human culture.[5]

Edwin McDermott clarifies this idea when he gives his understanding of the role of the Catholic school teacher. "Teaching is part of the ambiguity of all human life, and if it is to be salvific, the teacher must be a good person."[6] McCormick concurs that the role of the Catholic school teacher involves a personal witness to the values of Jesus Christ, even in the midst of academic and professional responsibility. He writes: "Can the mandates of the pastoral *To Teach As Jesus Did*, in itself a call to accountability, be reconciled with the inescapable bureaucratic requirements that befall diocesan school administrators, and ultimately, the crucial link in this chain, today's Catholic teacher? The answer is, and must be, yes."[7]

However, even when teachers in Catholic schools are respected and receive support and assistance from administrators, situations arise where the very goal of the Catholic school is in jeopardy. For one teacher, time may be a serious constraint. That teacher is unable to prepare properly lessons that will help students be formed according to the gospels transmitted through the Catholic church while responding to the many other demands made on limited time. Or, perhaps the problem is more personal, related to the expectation for living publicly according to the beliefs of the Catholic church.

Whatever the problem, when it is determined by administrators that there is no movement toward a solution, the teacher involved in such a situation is ineffective and termination should be considered. It is precisely because the Catholic church clearly defines and greatly values the contribution of the Catholic school teacher that the process of termination is only done after a long and just process. It is also done in such a way that the dignity and respect due to the teacher is preserved.

The Catholic church has had a long tradition of fidelity to justice. Over the centuries, the concept of justice as understood in the gospels has become more clearly defined. In 1891 Pope Leo XIII wrote *Rerum Novarum* (On the Condition of Labor) in which he tried to provide guidelines for Christian workers. He called for equity in bargaining and exchange. Workers, he stressed, should have the opportunity to form unions and to protect their rights. In his 1931 encyclical *Quadragesimo Anno* (On Restructuring the Social Order), Pius XI supports Pope Leo's defense of worker rights. He states that anyone who works must be given a living wage and that workers have a right to share in the profits of the organization.

In 1961, Pope John XIII wrote *Mater et Magistra* (Christianity and Social Progress) where he supported the rights of workers to full participation in industry decision-making. His second major encyclical on justice, *Pacem in Terris* (Peace on Earth), begins with a general listing of the rights of all human beings. One of these is the right to work in order to obtain and maintain a decent life. The right of due process is strongly implied in this text. In other church documents, including the Vatican II document, *Gaudium et Spes* (The Church in the Modern World), Pope Paul VI's encyclicals, *Populorum Progressio* (On the Development of People 1967), and *Octagesima Advaniens* (A Call to Action 1971), human rights and the dignity of human persons are systematically defined for local, state, national, international and global levels of society.

In *Justice in the World*, a pastoral letter written by American bishops in 1971, the rights of those who serve the church are clearly promoted. The right to due process for such people is clearly defined and all are encouraged to fight injustice in all forms. Pope John Paul II in his 1979 encyclical, *Redemptor Hominis* (Redeemer of Man), and in his many speeches urges all people to work for justice in labor practices and other situations, especially for the poor.

TERMINATION AND DUE PROCESS

Within the most recent pastoral by the American bishops, *Catholic School Teaching and the United States Economy*, the support of the church for the rights of workers is stated in decisive language. All are expected to observe civil laws concerning labor, one of which is due process.

Thus, while non-governmental agencies, including Catholic schools are not mandated to follow due process procedures by law, once due process is established it must be followed. Where specific due process procedures are not clearly designated, any situation which arises involving a labor-management dispute between Catholic school administrators and teachers should be solved by adherence to the teachings of the church on justice. There are two types of due process to be considered in issues of termination—substantive and procedural. Substantive due process refers to a liberty or property interest. An example of a liberty interest would be the protection of a teacher's reputation relative to future employment. An expectation of continued employment for the teacher is a property interest. Procedural due process protects a teacher from arbitrary actions by administrators or public officials.

DISMISSAL PROCEDURES

Teachers are terminated for different reasons. One cause for termination is reduction in force. Most commonly it is the result of declining enrollment, financial crises or changes in the educational program. Written policies for a reduction in force should be given to all teachers as a part of school policies. When it becomes necessary to implement such a plan, all teachers should be treated fairly and terminations should be carried out according to established policies.

The following suggested steps, while written for public schools, can easily be applied to Catholic schools where there is a need for reduction in force (R.I.F.)

1. Make your position on R.I.F. clear to both employees and the community; explain the current enrollment, financial, and employment picture.
2. Explain what you have done to keep R.I.F. to a minimum.
3. Explain the board's official policy on R.I.F.; be sure this policy is within state law and federal legislation.
4. Possibly appoint a task force on declining enrollments to gather information and act as a buffer between the board and the problem.[8]
5. Be sure that teachers are treated fairly and are suspended for the reasons stated. The American Association of School Administrators suggests:
   a. obtaining legal advice to help in wording the notice and in making sure deadlines are met
   b. adding a less formal message within the letter
   c. meeting with the staff who may be affected by R.I.F.
   d. issuing letters by registered mail, detailing a possible suspension
   e. issuing letters of actual suspension by registered mail.[9]
      These procedures display a genuine concern for the teachers who face suspensions or termination which are consistent with acceptable policies for the Catholic schools. Schools need procedures that protect the teacher and the school, including evaluation and termination.

The following four steps are typical of those which should be part of an evaluation process:

1. The teacher must be aware of the expected performance standards.
2. The teacher should participate in formative and summative evaluations and receive feedback on strengths and weaknesses.
3. Sufficient help must have been given to the teacher in order to correct an unacceptable performance.
4. A reasonable time for the teacher's improvement should have been designated.[10]

Five circumstances that should be present in any consideration of termination proceedings are:

1. Persistent nature of the difficulties
2. Repeated warnings
3. Frequent assistance
4. Close supervision
5. Normal and ordinary working conditions.[11]

When teachers have one year contracts, schools sometimes terminate teachers by simply not renewing the contract. While this action is perfectly legal, schools need to examine the justice and propriety of this kind of action. Without some kind of redress, teachers have little or no possibility for equitable treatment.

Any termination procedure needs to be conducted properly. The following simple steps provide guidelines for the process:

1. Have a good evaluation process.
2. Build your case. Document.
3. Make the recommendation to terminate.
4. Notify the teacher.
5. Prepare for the hearing.
6. Prepare for the oral review of the situation.
7. Live with the final outcome.[12]

There may not be a need in all Catholic schools to complete steps five and six, but in schools where teachers are represented in a collective bargaining agreement with administrators or in schools where termination procedures are established, this sequential process or one similar to it should be followed. Regardless of local policies, the Catholic school administrator must be knowledgeable concerning the legal and ethical components of the process as all teachers deserve the "letter and the spirit" of due process.

While each state lists specific reasons which are cause for dismissal, there are some reasons which are generally cited in all states. Most of these causes are serious enough that they warrant immediate action. In the public school setting, such charges would be presented at an official hearing and the teacher would be terminated once proof of the charges has been established. Whenever a serious situation such as those listed below exists in a Catholic school, similar prompt action should be taken.

The following causes are those for which no waiting period for possible correction is extended to the teacher.

One of these situations is neglect of duty which is equated with failing to act as a prudent person when supervising students or providing instruction on the operation of equipment. Another charge is immorality, including sexual immorality, abusive language in the classroom, dishonesty, falsifying records, stealing or cheating. Another is misconduct, which includes conviction of a felony or a crime. In Catholic schools, there is an additional serious charge. In most diocesan policy handbooks, there is a clear statement about the expectation of the Catholic school teacher to live in conformity with the laws and teaching of the Catholic church. When a teacher by his or her actions publicly contradicts church doctrines or regulations, the teacher may be dismissed immediately. These and other similarly serious charges cannot be tolerated in a Catholic education setting.

Only charges of insubordination, incompetency or inefficiency provide an opportunity for a waiting period in which the undesirable behavior may be corrected. By reviewing the specifics of the situation a charge of insubordination can be either affirmed or negated without extreme difficulty. When the charge is one of incompetence, identifying and clarifying this inadequacy becomes more difficult and is closely associated with a program of regular supervision and evaluation.

EVALUATION: FORMATIVE AND SUMMATIVE

In discussing supervision and evaluation practices, an important distinction must be made between formative and summative evaluation. Summative evaluation is a decision made about a teacher's performance, often in relation to such varied personnel decisions as teacher assignments, teacher transfers to other grade levels or subject areas, and to teacher termination. In many instances, a summative evaluation is done in compliance with officials outside the local school, whether local or diocesan. There is a continuing need for summative evaluation. Formative evaluation is used to improve a person's teaching skills through an ongoing process of observation where the supervisor gives pertinent feedback to the teacher on a regular basis. The primary focus in formative evaluation is the improvement of instruction.

Today, teacher accountability is a favorite topic at most educational gatherings. Within the evaluation process, it is important to preserve the rights of all educators. However, the improvement of instruction must remain the goal and primary reason for evaluation. In reference to legal reviews of teacher dismissal cases, McGreal writes:

There is no legal suggestion as to what the major purpose of evaluation should be, what data must be collected, what criteria be used, or what limits should be set on the level of teacher involvement. Obviously, it would be to the district's advantage to be sure that local evaluation procedures do not violate due process safeguards. But it should be made clear that evaluation systems can provide these protections and still be built with the primary focus on the improvement of instruction.[13]

Many different methods of evaluation are used by administrators and central office supervisory personnel. Some emphasize a review of standard criteria in areas pertinent to education, such as knowledge of subject matter or classroom management. Often a checklist with the criteria listed is used during or after a period of classroom observation and a teacher is judged on how well he or she attains an acceptable criterion or rating.

Methods that emphasize goal-setting have become widely used in recent years. This method evolves around an individual teacher's educational goals, which are frequently formulated at the beginning of a school year. A third method is clinical supervision where the teacher and supervisor meet to prepare and evaluate the lesson. A pre-conference, classroom observation, and post-conference, along with analysis on the part of the supervisor, form the basic components of this experience. These and other valid evaluation models are beneficial in as much as they ultimately strengthen the instructional program. What is important is that supervision is done on a regular basis as part of an established evaluation process and that written records are kept of the supervisory sessions.

Supervisory conferences have two discrete functions. The most important conference function is promotion of the teacher's growth in effective instruction. Conferences designed to improve instruction must be both diagnostic and prescriptive and are most accurately labeled instructional conferences. A secondary function of a supervisory conference is evaluation. The objective of an evaluative conference is that a teacher's placement on a continuum from unsatisfactory to outstanding will be established and the teacher will have the opportunity to examine the evidence of many instructional conferences.[14]

A good evaluation process will improve the instructional skills of all teachers through regular formative and occasional summative evaluation. Yet teachers have varied levels of professional expertise. To respond to the educational needs of teachers with their varied backgrounds, supervisors frequently assume different roles using directive, collaborative, and non-directive models with the teachers. Carl Glickman defines these models as follows: directive models call for the supervisor to be an enforcer of standards of teacher behaviors, to model and direct and measure proficiency levels; collaborative models involve the supervisor and the teacher as equal partners in the contracting of mutually planned changes; non-directive models enlist the support of the supervisor as a nonjudgmental clarifier, and encourager of decisions made by the teacher.[15]

TENURE

A consideration of the professional levels of teachers leads to a natural division of teachers for supervisory purposes into tenured and nontenured teachers. Diocesan handbooks clearly define the meanings of the terms tenured and nontenured. They differ from the uses of the terms in public schools. Tenured status in a Catholic school generally means that a teacher, after a designated period such as three successive years, should expect to have his or her contract renewed each year. In Catholic schools as in public schools, the supervisional focus for tenured teachers is the improvement of instruction through a refining of their teaching skills. Tenured teachers should be active participants in defining their own educational goals which are then agreed to by the supervisor. Any collection of data from the observation of tenured teachers should relate to these established goals.

While the supervisor also focuses on the improvement of instruction, the evaluation of nontenured teachers is to determine whether or not they will be retained in the school for the following year. The observations should be more frequent for nontenured teachers, at least once each semester. These may be formative in nature, but the final evaluation is a summative one.

For nontenured teachers the period of time previous to achieving tenured status is sometimes referred to as a probationary period. During this period, teachers may be given an annual contract, sometimes referred to as a spring-notification contract. With this annual contract, continued employment is contingent upon the teacher's being offered a new annual contract. If the contract is not to be renewed after the probationary period, the teacher is notified several months in advance of the expiration date so that new employment may be sought. When a probationary contract is not renewed, the teacher is dismissed and has no right to stated reasons for dismissal or to a hearing. If a teacher with an annual contract is dismissed before that contract has expired, school officials are responsible for documentation to show that the dismissal was not arbitrary and that it was done for a just cause.

DOCUMENTATION, RECOMMENDATION, NOTIFICATION

In Catholic schools, it is usually the administrator working with the pastor who makes the final decision to terminate a teacher. The opportunity for input from an advisory school committee may be provided by the principal and/or the pastor. It is important that any established diocesan policies regarding teacher termination be carefully followed by the administrator. When there is a serious possibility of the dismissal of a teacher, regular communication with the diocesan office of education is also essential to ensure diocesan support in this sensitive situation. Throughout a dismissal process, justice and fairness should be evident.

The guidelines which follow describe the initial steps in a termination process in the public sector. These steps ensure the public school teacher the right of due process. The Catholic school administrator should be aware of these legal requirements for teacher dismissal in the public school and where possible incorporate those points that are applicable in the termination process in a Catholic school. In the final stages of an unsuccessful evaluation process, the principal should be in communication with the superintendent. When it becomes evident that, after a designated period of time in which to correct deficiencies, even after repeated unsatisfactory evaluations, regular assistance from the principal and written warnings about the deficiencies, the tenured teacher's shortcomings will not improve, the principal initiates the formal process of dismissal. Once a decision has been made by the administrator that a tenured teacher should be recommended for termination, the work of evaluation over many months and the documentation of that evaluation process becomes a primary consideration. The following guidelines should be followed in organizing documented evidence:

In the text of all correspondence, there should be the following:
1. Give the dates of any work that was observed.
2. State an assistance offered and/or suggestions made.
3. Give an exact description of the dissatisfaction with performance.
4. State the nature of the action being recommended (withholding of increment, termination of services, etc.).
5. Keep the tone emotionally antiseptic. Diatribes or "loaded language" undercut the whole process.
6. Make copies properly; send to all persons who need to be informed.

7. Cause all correspondence to be receipted either via registered mail or by office signature.
8. Prepare a full and complete folder of all pertinent materials; such folder to be available for duplication at the proper legal moment. Materials therein should include all written classroom observations, annual evaluations, interim memoranda, letters, summaries of conferences.
9. DO NOT introduce written material that the teacher has not received. As a matter of fact, such material should not even exist.

When deciding whether or not to include selected pieces of information as documentation, the following standards should be considered:

1. Specific in nature. General charges carry little weight. Factual evidence of specific deficiencies in performance competencies and job related conduct must be presented.
2. Extensive in scope. An isolated case does not ordinarily constitute sufficient evidence except under unusual and extensive circumstances; a number of instances illustrating the problem must be submitted.
3. Recorded. All specific charges should be backed up by written statements made by the observer immediately after the various times the deficiencies were actually observed. In addition, all occasions where assistance is given or discipline or counseling sessions are held, should be made a matter of record. It is crucial that necessary information not only be recorded, but properly recorded. Properly recording means: entering appropriate dates and times, stating complete names of involved people, obtaining signatures of appropriate parties, listing of witnesses, notarizing statements, verifying by witnesses that the statements they signed contained true and correct information.
4. Original drafts. Written evidence presented at dismissal hearings of original drafts made at the time of, or immediately following the observation of performance (or conference), carry more weight than that reorganized or copied at a later date to prepare for a hearing. When all of the documentation has been gathered, the formal process of recommending a teacher for dismissal is initiated with the first step, preparing the statement of the reasons for dismissal. It must be carefully worded and the specific charges should be from those listed in each states' pertinent laws on dismissal.

Only issues previously discussed with the teacher and for which he or she has had ample warning and sufficient time for correction should be included in the statement of charges. Charges should refer to and quote from the written communication available from earlier observation and supervision sessions. When the concise statement of charges is complete, and accompanied by documented evidence which can be verified by testimony, it is sent to the superintendent who then makes a recommendation for dismissal of the teacher.

This recommendation for dismissal is the cause for a series of steps to be initiated:

1. The administrator in charge of the dismissal case asks the school board, on the recommendation of the superintendent, to consider the dismissal of the tenured teacher.
2. The board agrees to do this and a date is set, usually at least 30 days in advance, when the board will vote on the recommended dismissal.
3. The teacher is then notified of the exact date of the scheduled board consideration. If the teacher does not ask for a hearing, that hearing takes place on the date designated by the board.[16]

The termination process in a Catholic school has similar components:

1. Statement of charges. This is a written notice of termination given to the teacher by the administrator. This notice is given only after an appropriate number of negative evaluations have been made by the administrator to the teacher.
2. Hearing. This is a formal discussion where the administrator informs the teacher that he or she will not be rehired.
3. Appeal. If the teacher does not accept the termination action, he or she can appeal it through a grievance procedure.

A grievance procedure usually involves a series of steps which should be carried out within a specific time limit. If either the administrator or the teacher fails to adhere to the time limit, this failure will, by mutual consent, have negative consequences for the offending party and the grievance procedure will be terminated. The final step in such a grievance procedure could be the establishment of a Grievance Review Committee. Diocesan personnel might serve on such a committee and the decision of this committee would be final.

HEARING AND FINAL OUTCOME

The dismissal hearing of a public school teacher is a formal legal exercise which ensures the teacher the right of due process. The right of due process in the final stages of termination should also be available to the Catholic school teacher.

While it is unlikely that a hearing in a Catholic school setting would ever include the detailed and minute steps of a public school hearing, a formal hearing is also beneficial to the Catholic school administrator who works for just solutions in terminations situations. This organized process is designed both to provide rights to the teacher and to strengthen the educational system by dismissing inadequate teachers. These are common goals with which Catholic school administrators can identify.

During the designated period of time before the hearing, the teacher has time to prepare a defense and to retain an attorney, if desired. (The school may also have an attorney present.) If it is requested, a copy of the dismissal charges must be given to the teacher. Any other pertinent documents, including information in the teacher's file, should also be given to the teacher upon request.

The administrator, who will assume the role of "prosecutor" during the hearings, should try to foresee the arguments that the teacher will present and prepare responses to this anticipated defense. If witnesses are necessary, they should be notified of the date and time of the hearing.

Any documents that will be used by the administrator during the hearing to defend the dismissal charges should be organized for easy selection from the rest of the evidence when presenting the evidence to the due process board. The administrator will then avoid having to sift through disorganized papers.

The arrangement of the room should reflect the formality of this situation with the board of education seated in a central place and the witnesses at a table across the room facing the board or whatever group will make the decision. At tables on either side of the board, the administrator and the teacher are seated. If the hearing is a public one, those present should be seated so that it is evident that they are not to interfere with the proceedings. A tape recording should be used to make a record of the proceedings or a court stenographer should be employed.

After agreeing to hear dismissal charges, it is important that members of the board have no communication with either the administrator or legal counsel except concerning procedural questions; these are asked by the board president. It is incorrect to seek advice about the case itself. The board alone decides the case. On the designated date, the board president reviews the rules for the hearing. These rules may be questioned by the administrator, the teacher, or each side's legal counsel. First, the administrator and then the teacher present evidence to support or reject the dismissal charges.

The board members listen to the evidence, asking questions only for clarification and not to dispute claims.

The administrator, the teacher, or the attorneys are permitted to ask questions at any time during the hearing for purposes of clarification. Both parties may call witnesses to represent their positions and these witnesses may be cross-examined.
examined.

The purpose of the due process hearings of this sort is to give teachers who have been cited for dismissal a chance to hear the evidence against them, to present their own defense and witnesses for their defense, and to give, if desired, a face-to-face appeal to the board. At the same time, administrators have the task of presenting, as clearly as possible, the reasons for dismissal.[17]

It is extremely important that the administrator remain calm and controlled when presenting the charges or responding to questions. The principal should always think before responding to questions and present clear concise information in language that is understandable to persons other than educators. Both body language and eye contact during the hearing are important aspects of the administrator's presentation. Grier agrees.

> The administration should emphasize important information more than one time and in more than one place during a hearing. Committee members are not always listening carefully or do not understand the importance of key information the first time it is presented.[18]

After both sides have had the opportunity to present any information that they wish to make known, the president of the board closes the hearing. If the hearing is not public, the teacher and the teacher's attorney will be asked to leave while the board deliberates the charges. Only at this time does the board hear the administration's recommendation. Board members may debate further before voting on the recommendation. If the board votes for dismissal, then the charges from the administration are accepted and the teacher is terminated. If the board rejects the charges, the teacher resumes normal employment and the administration is left to evaluate whether or not some aspect of the preparations were not properly executed. If administrators understand the steps in the dismissal process, but also the importance of regular formative and summative evaluation, then teachers, supervisors, and administrators, working together, will strengthen the educational program which is an ultimate goal.

Catholic school teachers are actively involved in the ministry of Catholic education. Dismissal of a Catholic school teacher should be carried out in justice, for a healthy, professional climate benefits everyone, especially the students.[19] The termination of a tenured teacher is a serious action which should be carried out only as a "last resort" and after other attempts at remediation have failed. The termination of a Catholic school teacher involves an additional burden, both because of the dedication of the majority of teachers in Catholic schools and also because of the special participation of Catholic school teachers in the teaching mission of the church.

The good policies and practices concerning the termination of teachers should facilitate the process of terminating a teacher when for a good and just cause it becomes necessary to do so. To help ensure that termination is a just process, certain previous actions should be taken by a school. The school's hiring, grievance, evaluation, and termination policies should be in writing, preferably in the faculty handbook. They should be in line with diocesan policies and should be reviewed by an attorney. Any agreements beyond the contract between teacher and principal should be in writing. Any changes to the contract should be written on the contract and initialed by both parties. These precautions help maintain justice and avoid unnecessary acrimony later.

SUMMARY

1. When reduction in force is probable, this matter should be personally discussed with any teacher who faces possible termination.
2. The teacher should have the right of due process.
3. A satisfactory evaluation process should be established and documented evidence of regular evaluations of the teacher in question should be available.
4. The teacher must have participated in a formative evaluation process where the principal or supervisor provided assistance in identified areas of need.
5. Non-tenured teachers who are not rehired after the probationary period have no right to a due process hearing.
6. The proceedings in a termination hearing should be specified.
7. The legal proceedings of teacher termination cases, which present the findings of the courts in specific situations, can clarify the essential elements in a successful teacher termination policy.

FOOTNOTES

1. Walter M. Abbott, S.J. (ed.) *The Documents of Vatican II* (New York: Guild Press, 1966), p. 643.

2. Sacred Congregation for Catholic Education, *The Catholic School* (Washington, D.C.: Office of Publishing Services, United States Catholic Conference, 1977), p. 9.

3. National Conference of Catholic Bishops, *To Teach As Jesus Did* (Washington, D.C.: Publications Office, U.S.C.C., 1973), p. 12.

4. Abbott, *Documents of Vatican II*, p. 647.

5. Catholic Bishops, *To Teach As Jesus Did*, p. 29.

6. Sacred Congregation, *The Catholic School*, p. 13.

7. *Ibid.*, p. 12.

8. Edwin J. McDermott, S.J. *Catholic Schools: A Vision in Progress* (Washington, D.C.: National Catholic Educational Association, 1981), p. 46.

9. Michael McCormick, "To Teach As Jesus Did: Accountability in Perspective," *Today's Catholic Teacher*, January, 1979, p. 22.

10. McDermott, *Catholic Schools*, p. 46.

11. M. Chester Nolte, "Follow These 'How To's' When you Must Cut Your Staff," *American School Board Journal*, 48 (July, 1976), pp. 27, 45.

12. Ben M. Harris et al. *Personnel Administration in Education.* (Boston: Allyn and Bacon, 1979), p. 269.

13. Walter St. John, "Documenting Your Case for Dismissal with Acceptable Evidence," *N.A.S.S.F. Bulletin*, October, 1983, pp. 105-106.

14. Robert J. Munnelly, "What you should know when your staff asks you for a teacher dismissal hearing," *American School Board Journal*, 170 (May, 1983), p. 26.

15. Jerry D. Peterson, "Termination Hearings: A B C's of Survival," *N.A.S.S.P. Bulletin*, December, 1982, p.83.

16. Thomas L. McGreal. *Successful Teacher Evaluation* (Alexandria, Va.: A.S.C.D., 1983), p. 3.

17. Madeline Hunter, "Six Types of Supervisory Conferences," *Educational Leadership*, 37 (February, 1980), p. 408.

18. Carl D. Glickman, "The Developmental Approach to Supervision," *Instructional Leadership*, 38 (November, 1980), p. 179.

19. William R. Hazard, "Tenure Laws in Theory and Practice," *Phi Delta Kappa* (March, 1975), p. 96.

20. William Goldstein & Joseph C. De Vita, *Successful School Communications* (New York: Parker Publishing Company, 1977), p. 166.

21. St. John, Documenting Your Case, p. 105.

22. Munnelly, Teacher Dismissal Hearing, p. 22.

23. Ronald W. Rebore. *Personnel Administration in Education* (Englewood Cliffs, N.J.: Prentice Hall, 1982), p. 206.

24. Munnelly, Teacher Dismissal Hearing, p. 23.

25. Terry B. Grier, "Review these do's and don't's for teacher dismissal hearings," *The Executive Educator,* 6 (October, 1984), p. 21.

26. *Public Schools of Missouri,* Department of Elementary and Secondary Education (Jefferson City, Missouri: The Department, 1979), pp. 114-116.

27. Ann B. Dolgin, "The Role of Supervision in Teacher Dismissal Cases," *N.A.S.S.P. Bulletin,* February, 1981, p. 21.

28. Nutter v. School Committee of Lowell, 359 N.E.2d, 962 5 Mass App. 77 (1977).

29. Platko v. Laurel Highlands School District, 410 A.2d 960, 49 Pa. Cmwlth. 210 (1980).

30 . Christopherson v. Spring Valley Elementary School District, 413 N.E.2d 199 90 III.App.3d 460 (1980).

31. Harris v. Mechanicville Central School District, 394 N.Y.S.2d 302 57 A.D. 2d 231 (1977).

32. Gieringer v. Center School District, 585 S.W. 2d 109 (Mo. Ct. App. 1979).

33. Board of Education, Mount Vernon Schools v. Shank, 542 S.W.2d 779 (Mo. 1976).

34. Bovino v. Board of School Directors of Indiana Area School District 377 A.2d 1284,32 Pa. Cmwlth. 105 (1977).

35. Maddox v. Clackamas County School District, 626 P.2d 924 51 Or. App. 639 (1981).

36. Board of Trustees of Billings School District v. Board of Personnel Appeals 604 P.2d 770 (Mo. 1979).

37. Cohoes City School District v. Cohoes Teachers Association, 390 N.Y.S.2d 53 (N.Y. 1976).

38. Jacob v. Board of Regents for Education 365 A.2d 430 117 R.I. (1976).

SUGGESTED READINGS

Harris, Ben., et al. *Personnel Administration in Education.* Boston: Allyn and Bacon, 1979. The text details clear descriptions of supervisory behavior with an emphasis on observation of instruction; observation forms are also presented.

McGreal, Thomas. *Successful Teacher Evaluation.* Alexandria, Va.: A.S.C.D., 1983. The author presents varied and current supervision models, comparing the strengths and weaknesses; evaluation forms for teacher observation are included.

Rebore, Ronald. *Personnel Administration in Education.* Englewood,

N.J.: Prentice-Hall, 1982. Models for sequentially developed termination procedures are presented including sections on appraisal, grievance procedures, collective bargaining and the legal ramifications of termination.

CHAPTER VI
IN JUSTICE, THE TIMES DEMAND DEVELOPMENT

by
Rev. Robert J. Yeager Ed.D.

Father Yeager is Vice President for Development at NCEA. In that position, he conducts development efforts for the association and directs a national training symposium in development issues for parishes and schools. A priest of the Diocese of Toledo, he served for 15 years as secondary school principal.

INTRODUCTION

Justice is the moral virtue which in classical philosophy is said to concentrate on the rational appetite of a human being which can go out to others, even to God. From the side of its object, justice does not do the limited personal work of controlling human passion, rather it escapes the personal in its concern for the good of another or for the good of the community. Human life is successful only to the degree to which human activity measures up to the rule of reason.

Much of modern day discussion about the promotion of justice would proceed more rapidly to a successful conclusion if it were remembered that obligations are the basic claim to rights. Justice is a social virtue and society is a whole of which the parts are the individual citizens. The relation of the parts to the whole is regulated by legal justice, the relation of the whole to its parts by distributive justice, and the relation of part to part, of person to person, by cumulative justice.

This very brief summary on the Catholic thinking on the virtue of justice points to the basic theology which underlies the work of development.

This chapter will define the concept of development, show differences between development and fund raising, and give suggestions for the implementation of development programs in elementary and secondary schools. This concept is not discussed as such in church documents, although responsible stewardship and good common sense have been spoken about in church circles for many years.

Many justice issues are involved when any development program is implemented.

WHAT IS DEVELOPMENT

The term development was first used by the late Thomas A. Gonser in 1923 at Northwestern University. It used was to describe a function in the university meaning "development of the whole institution." It was never used as a synonym for fund raising.

Over the years others expanded this concept. Today, development is explained by the firm of Gonser Gerber Tinker Stuhr as:

> ...the concept that holds that the highest destiny of an institution can be realized only by a total effort on the part of the entire institution to analyze its educational philosophy, mission, and activities, to crystallize its objectives, project them into the future, and continually follow through to see that the objectives are realized.[1]

The development concept implies and demands:

1. An all-institutional approach.
2. Emphasis on the school's mission.
3. Institutional planning (long range with short term goals to fulfill its mission).
4. Proper placing of the development function in the administrative structure as well as leadership in development on the board of trustees.
5. Well defined development goals each year and a written plan to reach the goals.
6. Primary emphasis on the students served by the school and on the donors who support the program.

MUCH MORE THAN FUND RAISING

While it may be true that programs will never be actualized without funds, it is even more true that many programs have been funded without sufficient planning toward a goal. Action and delivery of "underplanned" programs only lead clients and supporters toward dissatisfaction with the institution. Fund raising, an important function in the development program, can never be mistaken for or equated with development. "Doing projects" may convince many in the short term that much is happening, but it will never replace serious planning and deliberate program execution.

Development in and for a Catholic school can never be merely fund raising because the gospel mandates that the church continue to "Go teach!" As schools are developed they must continue to create opportunities for learning not only for their students, but also for students' parents, grandparents and others in the Catholic community who have an interest in its educational endeavor.

Development work in Catholic schools calls for the highest ethical policies and their rigid enforcement. This mandate stems not only from the professional nature of development work, but also from the gospel mandate for justice and honesty. Catholic development work fails when it does not realize the breadth of the calling either of the school or of the development officer. A Catholic development officer hardly exists for only a school or a parish — he or she is called to make the message of Jesus more concrete in the lives of all those who are touched. The development officer is the minister of the word. Such a position may never be denigrated to the level of mere "fund raising." Jesus came with enthusiasm—not money. The spirit produced the material objects that were needed for his ministry among human beings.

There is ample evidence of this same kind of calling in the modern world. Many people are driven away from a gospel-oriented project when the financial aspects of it are discussed too early or without the creation of sufficient enthusiasm for shared decision making throughout the execution of the project.

Development is one of the main administrative functions of a school. Many Catholic schools face the financial and enrollment problems they do today because they have not realized over a period of time how important development is. Much of the administrator's time is spent in curricular and athletic areas. Catholics have long stood behind the banner of the Council of Baltimore which mandated that parents send children to Catholic schools under pain of sin and deprivation of the sacraments. It takes no learned guru to predict the kind of reverse effect this type of motivation has when it is removed. Still, this is not a time for hand wringing, but a time to admit that this approach will hardly meet the needs of the Catholic community today. Now is the time for Catholic schools to use resources of time, personnel, and finances to make development an integral part of the administration.

Catholic schools owe a debt in justice to parents and students to assure them that the administration will concern itself with the following areas:

1. Excellence in the academic areas;
2. Expansion and responsible management in student activities, with at least as much effort expended in the fine arts as in athletics;

3. Establishment of development programs which encourage and demand long-range, people-intensive planning;
4. Improvement in business affairs, with budgets well planned and reporting done to concerned publics on a regular basis.

The time is past when the number of teachers can be determined by taking the total number of children involved in a program, dividing by 30 or 35 and placing that many students in a classroom. The time is likewise past when teachers can be paid according to the lowest scale because it is argued that no additional funds are available. At the very least Catholic schools must address the psychological implications of low pay to teachers.

One might make an argument that there are more administrative functions to be added to the four that are listed, but there must be these four as a minimum in any Catholic school. This minimum is cited here in an attempt to point out that development is so much more than fund raising and that development is of equal importance with academic excellence, student services, and good business functioning.

PURPOSE

"Why have a development program?" The material presented above addresses part of the answer to this question. One should not take the approach that the beginning of a development program seems overwhelming and therefore should not be begun. A full development program will not be instantaneously operational. In fact, development programs always have room to grow and improve. Many of the concepts introduced into development are not terribly profound, but simply must be done in an ordered and administratively responsible manner. Development requires much more repetitive work than ingenious momentary insights. If one just does the tasks professionally over a period of time, the institution will be improved in its responsibility to bring the gospel message.

The purposes and therefore the criteria for measurement of an effective development program are:
1. To obtain greater acceptance for the institution from its major publics.
2. To obtain more participants of the quality and quantity that the institution desires. If the institution is a school, this purpose is obvious. However, the same can be said of any educational program in a parish. This same concept might even be used to obtain more members of a parish congregation.

3. To secure additional funds for institutional programs through:
   a. the annual fund for current operations;
   b. specific capital projects;
   c. major capital effort;
   d. funds from deferred giving or estate planning.
4. To "en-spirit" all those who touch the institution to an enthusiasm and sharing of institutional goals in a very practical way. The Catholic development program should move people away from the "obligation" mentality and into the arena of those who are delighted to be a part of the people of God called to "Go Teach!" While obligation has some undesirable aspects to it, being called to bring Jesus to others is a concrete way of inviting others to use their time, talent, and treasure in a manner which has meaningful religious effects.
5. To provide the arena in which networking can take place among all the individuals who share in a common institutional goal. It is amazing how much an institution is moved forward when informal exchanges occur through parties interested in institutional goals, but who have no forum in which to meet.
6. To provide materials and programs in which publics may obtain a better understanding of the role played by this institution within the community, the educational community, the church community. We must begin to present the relationship of individual Catholic educational institutions to other institutions. This relationship is poorly understood by the Catholic community. The informational purpose of development should assist in building the understanding component of the total development effort.

TRADITIONAL FUND RAISING

In contrast to a comprehensive development program, the traditional fund-raising campaign has one phase.[2] Its purpose is to raise a specific sum of money from all the publics of the parish for the same project, normally a capital project or a combination of projects. Once the total sum has been set, there is intensive and general solicitation over a specific period of time to meet the goal. The emphasis is on getting all the publics to give to the common goal and to make definite commitments within the set period.

One advantage of this traditional fund-raising approach is that there is impetus to set up an organization to solicit prospects within a definite period of time for a definite monetary goal. An institution is forced to be specific. Another advantage is the urgency and pressure of reaching the goal within the set period.

Among the problems of the fund-raising campaign are:

The urgency of reaching the goal may induce solicitors to put undue pressure on their prospects, which rarely produces major gifts.

A donor may be forced to give a token amount without ever really being sold on the program of the institution itself.

The campaign is not geared to train both volunteers and staff members in a continuous program. The emphasis is on a crash effort.

When the campaign is over, there is often little effort to transfer the benefits gained into a sustained, long-range program.

An intensive solicitation effort, with its concentration on travel, dinners, campaign accessories, and additional staff, is often very expensive.

A specific capital campaign may fail to attain its goal, thus creating a lack of confidence in the institution by its investors and friends.

ADVANTAGES OF COMPREHENSIVE PROGRAM

A comprehensive long-range development program has many advantages:

A carefully worked out development program takes a look at all methods of the financing for parish (Sunday offering, income from auxiliary activities, endowment income economies achieved by more efficient operation, cooperation with other parishes, loans, annual gifts, capital gifts, deferred gifts) rather than looking only at the capital gifts needed within a definite period.

A well-thought-out development program produces an academic blueprint which gives a parish a sense of direction for many years.

Continuity in fundraising over the years is provided by building in an annual program for current operations, a sustained effort to obtain specific capital projects, a continuous program of obtaining funds through estate planning, and from time to time scheduling an intensive effort to finish up a major capital project.

The training and use of both volunteers and staff members on a continuing basis year after year is most helpful.

WHO IS THE DEVELOPMENT PERSON?

The responsibility for development activity should be given to a staff member. Since the principal or head of a program has a definitive role to play in the development effort, this is not a role where the principal can wear two hats. The development officer should not be the principal, although at the outset of a program the principal may perform certain of the development functions until the development officer is in place. In the earliest stages of moving toward development, the principal may well guide volunteers in such activities as organizing the data about the school or researching the names and current addresses of the alumni.

For the long term, however, the principal should not be the development officer, as the principal has his or her own role to play in a total development effort. For the principal to accept both positions of principal and Vice Principal for Development weakens the effectiveness of each position as the publics dealt with will be hard pressed to recognize the appropriate "hat" at the proper time. Much development work is successful because of personal interactions. These dynamics can hardly occur between "hats" worn by one person!

Who is the development person? This person is the one to whom development means new institutional resources who will increase the status of the development area. Development is not a profession, but does require a professional. A profession is a calling requiring specialized knowledge, often preceded by long and intensive academic preparation.

A professional is one who:
1. practices a full time occupation;
2. feels a deep commitment to his or her calling and has deep feelings about the institutional goals which he or she is responsible for advancing;
3. possesses knowledge and skills based on education and special training, which ideally will be of exceptional duration and perhaps exceptional difficulty, in the following areas:
   a. communications
   b. marketing
   c. management
   d. direct mail
   e. public relations
   f. power structure
   g. facilitation
   h. ombudsmanship for donor
   i. education
   j. sales
4. is service oriented;

5. enjoys considerable autonomy restrained by responsibility;
6. endeavors to protect and enhance the interests and status of the occupation, especially through active participation in professional organizations and accreditation;
7. enjoys acceptance and status among other professionals.

QUALIFICATIONS OF A GOOD DEVELOPMENT OFFICER

The qualifications of a good development officer can be outlined in the following manner:

1. Shows integrity
   a. personal—meets all personal qualifications for all other members of the school staff
   b. professional
   c. integrity to the school
2. Shows understanding and enthusiasm for the school.
   This suggests that the development officer will continue to learn about institutional growth through participation as a regular faculty member in faculty meetings, liturgical events, athletic and extra-curricular events.
3. Has the ability to be an extension of the office of the principal especially by representing the principal's aims and objectives at all meetings and activities.
4. Accepts responsibility with all that implies in terms of reporting on outcome of activities.
5. Establishes high standards for self and others.
6. Is a self starter—must have considerable personal initiative which operates within general institutional goals.
7. Is motivated personally and can motivate others. In a word the development officer must be a POSITIVE PERSON.
8. Can prepare a personal schedule and work up to it. Must also be able to supervise schedules of those working with the development office.
9. Is in robust health. Must have the ability to work hard for long periods of time; practice good eating and rest habits.
10. Has the ability to communicate, especially through the written word. Must present a good appearance to those who will be met personally.
11. Has an outgoing personality with a reasonable ability to get along with others.
12. Has a sense of timing and appropriateness for various behaviors.

13. Can numerate as well as literate which presupposes a habit of reading.
14. Has experience in development or some related activities.

Development begins with the Board of Education. Admittedly the principal and in the case of parish schools the pastor also play very important parts, but the school board must be active from the very moment that development is conceived in a local school. Development is one of the main administrative functions of an institution and should be one of the main administrative divisions.

The rapid growth of development programs in Catholic schools in recent years has focused attention on the key role of the development director in obtaining new resources.

Development has come a long way from the old-fashioned stereotype of fund raising. Many outstanding men and women have chosen development for their careers. It is a field that is tremendously important, for development is the administrative function of the school which is concerned with obtaining new resources. The school's chances for survival and growth depend on these new resources which include: increased acceptance with the school's important publics; more funds for current operations and capital growth; and an adequate quantity of the kind and quality of students the school wishes to serve.

The director of a development program in a Catholic elementary or high school must be more than a fund raiser. To succeed in his job the development officer must also be an

Educator: Above all, the development director must understand education, must believe in the educational purposes of the school, must know thoroughly the educational programs his institution is endeavoring to inaugurate or maintain, and be able to formulate and direct continuing efforts to obtain support for these programs.

Manager: In the first place, the development officer is a line officer, managing his or her own own area of operations, familiar with management techniques and their operation in an educational institution.

Communicator: Development concerns the cultivation and obtaining of acceptance and support from the publics vital to an institution. No program of cultivation and fund raising will work without a knowledge of how to communicate with these publics. The press, radio, television, personal contacts, publication, exhibits, displays, speeches, meetings, events, open houses, all of these and countless other means of communication are integral parts of a development program. The director must be able to communicate effectively.

Researcher: Too many development programs get launched without necessary research concerning the basic problems, past history, the potential for support, and the factors which will affect the outcome. Similarly, evaluation is a technique used all too sparingly in development programs. Too many projects and procedures are continued each year without adequate evidence as to their effectiveness. The development director should understand the techniques and procedures of research and evaluation and bring them to bear on the local program.

Leader: In addition to the leadership expected from members of school boards, the development director must be a leader too. While he or she is responsible to the principal and as a staff member carries out the policies established by the school board, the director must personally take the lead in initiative, action, perseverence, follow through, and painstaking attention to details. The director must be a self starter, a pace setter, and an establisher of high standards. A development director must lead the staff as well as the volunteers whom he or she recruits, trains, and works with, in vision, dedication, personal integrity and plain hard work. The high turnover rate among development directors is disturbing. Not all of it, however, is because the development director is following the lure of higher salaries elsewhere. Some schools cannot retain their development directors because of:

1. Misunderstanding on the part of the institution concerning the development director's role and proper goals;
2. Lack of a clear cut job description;
3. Lack of clear direction on the part of the pastor, principal and/or board of education;
4. Lack of proper training;
5. Salaries which are too low, with no realistic consideration of the market;
6. Salaries which are too high, making them out of line with those of other administrative or teaching personnel, thus creating internal problems.

SOURCES OF DEVELOPMENT DIRECTORS

The question is often asked, "Where should I look for a director of development?" Effective development directors in Catholic schools have come from many sources. Among these are:

1. alumni and parents. These persons are most familiar with and

usually most dedicated to the aims of the school.

2. the faculty of the school. Do not forget to begin at home. If some-one can be found that already knows and understands the school's mission and goals, so much the better.

3. other Catholic schools either inside or outside the diocese. Often family or other personal reasons make a change of location necessary.

4. social agencies, such as the Boy Scouts, Girls Scouts, Red Cross, Salvation Army and charitable organizations. Retired Catholic business people who have a background in this type of related work are often anxious to be doing something. They are excited when asked to be of help to the school.

5. the armed forces. A good source for experienced and able people can be found here.

UNDERESTIMATED COMPONENTS

Three often underestimated components of the development program are planning, public relations and recruitment of students. The tradition of commitment to education in the church mandates a commitment by pastors, principals, and others to continuing education within the church ministry. The earlier commitment of people's time, talent, and financial resources demand in justice that those current-ly in parish positions use development tools to enhance educational programs.

STRATEGIC PLANNING

Pastors, principals, school board members and others interested in a Catholic school should ask themselves what is the status on long-range planning at their parish school. They should know how recent-ly the long-range plan has been made, if indeed one is in place, and whether the current plan is on schedule. If no plan exists one needs to be created. Any existing plan should be reviewed and brought up to date.

Chances are there is a plan somewhere to do something. Planning has been on the agenda for decades. While longer planning periods were popular some time ago, it has recently been more practical to have a 5-year plan and to bring it up to date at the end of each fiscal year.

The problem in Catholic schools today is that much earlier plann-ing was done for the purpose of building new buildings, building new faculty and implementing new programs. During the 1960's, a period of rapid growth, planning mainly consisted of balancing the annual budget and putting on some sort of fund-raising event to cover any short-fall that existed. Many parishes had such a corporate commitment to educate their children that they often charged no tuition.

STRATEGIC AND COMPREHENSIVE PLANNING

During this time of limited enrollment possibilities, increased competition for students and financial support, and abrupt changes in the environment and in clientele, planning is more crucial than ever. Schools need to follow the lead of business and industry in embarking on comprehensive and strategic planning.

John S. Toll, President of the University of Maryland, characterizes strategic planning as concentrating "on the changing environment surrounding one's institution as much as it pays attention to internal hopes and needs. It analyzes the threats and opportunities from the emerging demography, technology, economic and financial trends, political and legal developments, international conditions, and the concerns for changing values and quality of life. It matches departmental and collegiate wish lists with the probable realities of the society that universities hope to serve. Strategic planning tries to find an appropriate strategy for forward movement and success, consistent with faculty initiative and goals."[2]

PLANNING FACILITATES ACTION

Whether it goes by the name of an educational long-range plan, or a master plan for institutional advancement, or strategic planning, or a blueprint for the future, the bottom line is a program of action to achieve the full potential for service of educational efforts. In fact, one of the meanings which Webster lists for blueprint is "a thoroughly plotted and coordinated program of action."

Such action can be assured, however, only when:

The planning is genuine and not just a back drop for fund raising.

The planning concentrates not only on internal goals and desires, but also on the changing outside environment, on human factors, on shifting markets, on society's requirements and expectations, and on the resources possible and available to the school today.

The planning is concerned with ideas and ideals, not just dollars.

The planning is done by the entire institution, not just the administration.

The planning gives many parts of the school, administration, faculty, staff, alumni, parents, students, community, and church leaders, an opportunity to work together. As President Toll said in *Change*, "Planning is a process of changing the attitudes, behavior, and work habits of people as much as it is a matter of cognitive ingenuity and shrewdness."

The planning becomes part of the "Case for Support" of the school.

An organization of volunteer workers is built which can understand, interpret, and market the institutional plan or blueprint to the key publics.

Strategic planning involves the entire institution, not just the administration because strategic planning or blueprinting requires total institutional study and analysis, many offices and groups must be involved.

Strategic planning in the parish school should be:
- Authorized by the Board of Education.
- Initiated by the administrator, with full approval and cooperation of the pastor.
- Referred to the board of education for approval of the general process of planning.
- Prepared by the administration, faculty and staff.
- Reviewed by many publics of the institution, including faculty, key leaders of the parish community, parents, as well as board of education and advisory boards.
- Approved in its final plan by the administration and board.
- Utilized by the development office with the help of volunteers to obtain financial support for the ideas, concepts and programs that the plan embraces.

THE INSTITUTION'S CASE STATEMENT

Once a consensus has been reached on the institutional plan, a case statement can be drawn up for use in communicating the planning, the institutional mission, and the programs and resources necessary to enable the institution to survive and fulfill its potential.

Most institutions today have or are working on "case statements." However, if the planning has thoroughly examined and considered the institution's markets, the opportunities and limitations present in today's environment and climate, future trends and how they will affect the school, the school's mission and thrust in the light of its purpose, resources, and the understanding and support it can obtain, then the case statement can be a brief and clear statement about:

The institution's mission, what it means to its community and constituencies and to all of society.

The programs of the institution and the directions the institution will take in the light of today's environment and trends to realize its aims.

The resources necessary to enable the school to maintain its programs, fulfill its aims, and serve society.

The importance to society of reaching the goals set by the school.

The results of strategic planning and the statement of the case for support of the school's mission and programs should be written and distributed in a concise, clear version to the institution's key publics.

Plans do no good if they are allowed to smolder in the files. They must be communicated. This should be part of the strategy of strategic planning.

PUBLIC RELATIONS

Many Catholic school and parish administrators come to the practice of planning from sheer necessity. Prior to Vatican Council II many went along according to the old pattern in the church. It was a boom time in Catholic education. There were no perceived public relations problems. Enter the Council as well as many of the social and economic uprisings in the United States and it became a very different world.

In the new reality nothing moves, or improves, or has money spent on it unless it is documented. Planning for public relations is not easy work. Only a quiet rigorous exercise will assure arrival at a public relations plan that fits your particular needs. A brief radio announcement here and several newspaper reports there about a school will not begin to convey to the community the goals of a local Catholic school.

A plan is a predetermined course of action. Planning is an intellectual process. It is a product of some degree of creative thinking on the part of the planners. Any worthwhile plan:

involves the future;

involves action;

involves an element of personal or organizational identification;

involves consensus and approval;

involves provisions for evaluation.

There is a distinction between a plan and a policy. A policy is a general guide to future decision-making intended to shape those decisions to maximize the contribution to the goals of the enterprise. A plan should fit with the guidelines of a policy but it is not policy.

The golden rule of planning is this: a planner accomplishes nothing until he or she communicates with and gains consensus from those persons who must approve the plan and those who must implement it.

Communication is the process of conveying meaning, including all of the procedures by which one mind affects another, choice of words, tone and volume of voice, and eye contact.

The critical first step in planning is an effective public relations program. Quite frankly, this is where the first good, honest sweat comes in. The development director must be willing to work to come up with a "statement of mission." A "statement of mission" describes what a person is trying to do and why that person is trying to do it. Why are they trying to do what he or she is trying to do? The next step is "priorities" within that mission — and these are best looked at in short-range fashion. They should be flexible and able to change as the situation changes.

Here is a sample statement of priorities. Priorities are those tasks that are chosen for one of two reasons: they are the most important things to do — or they are the things that are most accomplishable at a specific time. All priorities ever established should further the mission of your office or operation.

The benefits of a statement of mission and priorities are numerous. A statement of mission:

1. Aids in explaining what to do and why you do it.
2. Helps explain what not to do and why. (Helps ward off persons who come with ideas that do not fit what is being done or why it is being done; or that fit the "mission" but not the set of "priorities" under which the project is functioning.)
3. Can aid significantly in securing adequate staffing and budgeting.
4. Keeps focusing, thinking and acting on target and serves as a constant check.

Once a person has struggled and successfully gotten down on paper a "Statement of Mission and Priorities," that person is ready to consider the more concrete steps of an effective public relations plan.

The next steps are:

1. Defining target audiences—

a. Who must be reached with news and information and other public relations strategies?

b. Why do you want to reach those particular persons or organizations?

c. What action do you want your target audiences to take?

d. What actions will indicate that your target audiences have taken the desired action?

2. Defining themes—

a. What message or messages do you want to transmit to your target audiences?

b. What are the most important facts in your message that need constant repetition so as to make a lasting impact on your target audiences?

3. Defining methodology—

a. The message or messages you wish to deliver highlighting the themes you wish to stress must be delivered to the target audience in a way that will elicit the response you desire.

b. Decision on forms of media best suited to deliver selected message to selected target audiences.

c. Decisions on other public relations techniques:

1. Speakers' Bureau

2. Editorial Board visits

3. Op-ed page pieces

4. Background sessions

4. Evaluation—The answers to four basic questions can help you determine the degree of success achieved by your public relations plan:

a. Did I aim at the right targets—the persons or organizations I wanted to influence?

b. Did my message suit my target audience?

c. Did I use the right delivery system?

d. Did my target audience or audiences do what I wanted it or them to do, indicating that my strategy had paid off?

The most important fact about this plan is that it can be used as an "umbrella plan" to guide everything being done, and it can be "miniaturized" to fit any particular public relations project you undertake. The best public relations plan ever devised will be worthless unless it is approved by one's superiors and it is truly adopted and followed by those who have to implement it. Planning for public relations is best carried out in a group setting where true professionals of equal training, ingenuity, and creativity can freely exchange ideas. It is important to get one's superiors to "sign off" on the plan, and it's a good idea to update them on the plan's progress personally or by memorandum. No public relations plan is going to succeed unless there is a commitment both to the organization for which the plan is devised and to the plan itself.

RECRUITMENT

No school can operate without students. Yet many Catholic elementary and secondary schools do not have an active recruitment program. In communities which have multiple Catholic schools a joint recruiting program should be considered. For people not closely tied to the Catholic Church, it is difficult to understand the independence of some Catholic schools.

An effective admissions/recruitment program is the first step toward the viability—or to put it bluntly—survival of the school in the 1980's. Recruitment is part of the school's overall program for its advancement. Just as important as effective fund raising and public relations is the admissions program.

A successful recruitment program which meets its goals each year helps the school:

move toward its full potential for service;
fulfill the educational aims for which it was founded;
maintain and enhance the quality of teaching and learning;
maintain high school morale especially among staff and students;
improve relations with the publics on which it depends for support;
balance its budget without which no school can long endure.

No program in the school so directly and immediately influences the life of the school than a successful—or unsuccessful—recruitment program. It is vital for a school to examine, evaluate and revise as necessary its efforts to obtain the kind and number of students it needs.

The pastor, principal, and perhaps a committee of the board of education may want to be part of the evaluation process for recruitment. They will evaluate:

- which goals were met and which were not, especially in regard to grade 1 and grade 9 entrants. (returning students and transfer students would also be considered);
- the effectiveness of those people who were actually involved in recruiting, whether paid or volunteer;
- individual activities which were mounted for recruitment, i.e., school visits, mail pieces, radio and tv advertising, etc.;
- support received from various administrators of parish and school;
- support from faculty and students;

- support from volunteer groups;
- the program being marketed
  a. academic program
  b. student activities including parish and liturgical involvement
  c. physical plant
  d. other factors—i.e., tuition, fees

A FINAL WORD

In a recent brochure announcing a development fund gift plan for Cardinal Newman High School, Most Reverend Mark J. Hurley, Bishop of Santa Rosa, California stated "the challenge for the future is clear: a development program is essential for survival." Time is a finite commodity in each Catholic community. For whatever reasons we have allowed the quality of our stewardship to lag in recent years. Catholic schools do not now have an infinite amount of time in which to reverse this back-sliding.

Unless the demands of justice are soon realized through comprehensive development efforts, Catholic educational institutions will be at a distinct disadvantage. Many of them may not survive such a period. Catholic schools and parishes are a major way the church preaches the gospel message. The message deserves the best possible delivery system that can be made available.

SUMMARY

1. Justice demands that obligations are the basic claim of rights.
2. Development is defined as total effort.
3. Development is quite different from fund raising. Each activity as a proper place, but should not be confused with the other.
4. A development program is a dynamic and gradually emerging reality.
5. Development activity should be the responsibility of one staff member. This is not to say that others are not involved in much of the work. The development officer should not be the chief operating officer, whether this is the pastor or principal.
6. A competent development officer comes with definite qualifications.
7. Successful development programs in schools show evidence of thorough planning, public relations and recruitment of students.
8. Strategic planning is the heart of any parish development program. Planning today differs from that of the 60's and needs to be not only strategic but also comprehensive.

9. The benefits of a statement of mission and priorities are numerous.

FOOTNOTES

Material presented in this chapter has been adapted from ideas and concepts on development presented in various issues of the *Bulletin on Public Relations and Development for Independent Schools* published by Gonser Gerber Tinker Stuhr, Chicago, Il. For some time Dr. Robert Stuhr, a partner in the firm, has been guiding national efforts to bring development to American Catholic elementary and secondary schools.

1. Robert L. Stuhr, *Bulletin on Public Relations and Development for Independent Schools*, Gonser Gerber Tinker Stuhr, Chicago, Il., June 1982, p. 1.

2. This material was first presented in *Pastors Development Newsletter*, Vol. 1 No. 1, May 1984, published by National Catholic Educational Association.

SUGGESTED READINGS

Bulletin on Public Relations & Development for Independent Schools. A bi-monthly publication, free for principals and chief development officers., Gonser Gerber Tinker Stuhr, Chicago.

Burke, Richard J., *Understanding and Implementing Development*, Development is much more than fund raising. Development includes understanding, commitment, involvement, planning, a statement of the case and funding. This publication presents practical suggestions which are now succeeding in numerous Catholic institutions., National Catholic Educational Association, Washington, D.C., 1984.

Burke, Richard J., Richard A. Fenchak, James A. Haudan, George Hofbauer, John A. Thomas, and Robert J. Yeager, *Elementary School Finance Manual*. This volume treats key financial areas that are the responsibility of the Catholic elementary school: Daily Financial Operations; The Annual Budget; Tuition; Long-Range Planning; Fundraising; and Steps Toward Development. It offers many examples of ready-to-use forms., National Catholic Educational Association, Washington, D.C., 1984.

Butler, Francis J., and Catherine E. Farrell, *Foundation Guide for Religious Grant Seekers*, Second Edition, This new edition of a standard classic is a must for anyone seeking assistance from foundations., Scholars Press, California, 1984.

Campbell, Cathy, SP, *Public Relations*. Planning and execution of a successful Public Relations program are essential to the success of Catholic institutions. Public Relations is made easy with the steps detailed in this booklet, which gives methods for use with all types of media and with all sizes of audience., National Catholic Educational Association, Washington, D.C., 1984.

Cutlip, Scott M., and Allen H. Center, *Effective Public Relations*, Fourth Edition. One of the standards upon which public relations is built. Prentice-Hall, Inc., New Jersey, 1982.

Greenleaf, Robert K., *Servant Leadership*. A valuable book for those interested in new models of leadership based on gospel values. Questions the transfer of industrial models to not-for-profit institutions. Paulist Press, New York, 1977.

Jarc, Jerry A., and Robert L. Stuhr, *Annual Fund—Estate Planning*. A comprehensive book filled with practical suggestions helpful in two major development areas. The Annual Fund Drive and the establishment of an Estate Planning Program can succeed by following the steps outlined by two nationally acclaimed authors., National Catholic Educational Association, Washington, D.C., 1984.

Whelan, Donald J. (ed.), *Handbook for Development Officers of Independent Schools*. The book offers a sample of the many skills that Catholic schools might learn from independent school practice. Council for Advancement and Support of Education, Virginia, 1980.

Yeager, Robert J., *The Case Statement*. How to use institutional philosophy, mission, long-range plans, programs, effects on the broader community and resources as the basis for making a Case Statement. Outlines and detailed suggestions to be used in the construction of a Case Statement. National Catholic Educational Association, Washington, D.C., 1984.

CHAPTER VII
COMPREHENSIVE DIOCESAN PERSONNEL POLICIES
by
Lois King Draina, Ed.D.

Lois Draina has been involved in Catholic education for over 23 years as a teacher, elementary and secondary principal, and as superintendent in the Diocese of Richmond, Virginia. While superintendent, she helped the diocese establish comprehensive personnel policies. She completed her doctoral studies in education in the areas of management and personnel.

INTRODUCTION

The teaching mission of the Catholic Church is competently served by the persons who minister in Christ's name. Their response to the mandate to preach the gospel message brings their sense of ministry within the church to fruition. Their spirit of service engenders a dedication which moves far beyond the more pedestrian understanding of "one's job." Finally, a minister within the church consistently seeks ways to teach and to prophesy in response to the call of the gospel:

> There is a variety of gifts but always the same spirit; there are all sorts of service to be done, but always the same Lord; working in all sorts of different ways in different people, it is the same God who is working in all of them. . . .One may have the gift of preaching with wisdom given him by the Spirit; another may have the gift of teaching given him by the same Spirit. . . .all these are the work of one and the same Spirit who distributes different gifts to different people as he chooses.
> (1Cor 12:4-11).

Two basic principles are operative and pervasive throughout Catholic social teaching: the inherent dignity of the human person and the idea of the common good. The Second Vatican Council stated emphatically that ". . .the beginning, the subject, and the goal of all institutions is and must be the human person."[1] Common good, understood within church tradition, is ". . .not so much the summation of the goods of individual citizens as it is a set of social conditions which facilitate human development. . . .It stands as a call

163

to responsibility whereby we are all required to work for the general welfare of the entire family."[2]

Herein lies the challenge, then, for both employee and employer as together they form a work-bond and meet personal and organizational goals and objectives. Herein lies the challenge to model to the public sector the abiding principles of personal liberty and justice. Herein lies the challenge of producing a comprehensive, clear, concise, and public delineation of policies regarding the rights, benefits, and responsibilities of both employee and employer. And herein lies an answer to the full development of a minister within the church.

CHURCH DOCUMENTATION

In 1971 the Synod of Bishops published *Justice in the World.* It presents a fundamental challenge to the understanding of the conditions of the world of work. The church preaches that work itself is inherently tied to social justice principles and to making life more human.

While the Church is bound to give witness to justice, she recognizes that anyone who ventures to speak to people about justice must first be just in their eyes. Hence we must undertake an examination of the modes of acting and of the possessions and life style found within the Church itself.

Within the Church rights must be preserved. No one should be deprived of his ordinary rights because he is associated with the Church in one way or another. Those who serve the Church by their labor, including priests and religious, should receive a sufficient livelihood and enjoy that social security which is customary in their region. Lay people should be given fair wages and a system of promotion. We reiterate the recommendation that lay people should exercise more important functions with regard to Church property and should share in its administration.[3]

In *Laborem Exercens (On Human Work),* Pope John II links closely the notion of personhood and work:

Man has to subdue the earth and dominate it, because as the "image of God" he is a person, a subjective being capable of acting in a planned and rational way, capable of deciding about himself, and with a tendency to self-realization. As a person, man is therefore the subject of work. As a person, he works, he performs various actions belonging to the work process; independently of their objective content, these actions must all serve to realize his humanity, to fulfill the calling to be a person that is his by reason of his very humanity.[4]

According to Father Donald McCarthy in his *Catholic Vision of Work in the World,*[5] the Catholic view of workers is one that "exalts the inestimable dignity of the human person, gifted with knowledge, conscience, and freedom by the Creator, and seeking the common good through social structures and relationships. The significance of work in the Catholic tradition is found in the fact that man is the subject of work. . . In this view labor belongs not to the state or to capital, but to the worker, whose individual wealth it is."

It is true that employment in a church-related institution, such as a Catholic school, raises issues not present in the typical industrial or commercial setting. Additionally, Catholic schools serve human needs and have always been church and tuition-supported institutions, characterized by a non-profit status. The majority of employees are now lay. At the same time that the institution called Catholic school maintains its truly religious dimension and its concern for the education of the whole child, some of its efforts must necessarily turn inward toward those who make these lofty goals a reality.

Employees in the "Christian community" share profoundly in the church's teaching mission. Social justice to all is the norm. Social encyclicals and mandates address dimensions of work life that commercial and industrial enterprises lack. Employees' needs and employees' rights are now more than ever in the forefront of current church dialogue.

Maintaining the Catholic institution's integrity while caring for and dignifying the rights and responsibilities of every worker within the institution calls for some new answers. Theological traditions, social encyclicals, or a reemphasis of the institution's mission cannot alone provide adequate solutions to the complex labor-management tensions inherent in human interactions, particularly in the workplace.

Creative thought might direct the Catholic educational institution to look toward a collaboratively and comprehensively designed set of policies and procedures that consistently and clearly benefit both the institution and the persons employed therein.

COMPREHENSIVE PERSONNEL POLICIES

Comprehensive personnel policies within a diocese or within a school system

1. recognize all men and women whose ministries have been therein authorized;

2. establish statements governing the hiring and just and equal treatment of all employees of the diocese or of the system, which would include competitive living wages, benefits and retirement commensurate with education, competency and job requirements;
3. clarify roles, relationships and lines of authority and accountability;
4. make public the rights and responsibilities of both employer and employee within the institution;
5. systematize and organize the potentially complex inter-relatedness of labor and management; and
6. accomplish their purpose in the light of the social teaching and the traditions of the church.

DEVELOPING EFFECTIVE POLICIES

From a general perspective, comprehensive personnel policies must be characterized by the following "effectiveness factors."

1. *Personal Ownership*: Every employee, from custodian to classroom teacher to superintendent to bishop, must take personal ownership of a manual of personnel policies. Each should assist in the development and implementation of policies and, most critically, maintain a clear understanding of rationale and related policy procedures.
2. *Wide Consultation*: Both management and labor have the right and responsibility to participate in the development of personnel policies if they are to be truly reflective and representative. Broad, multi-level, and objective consultation processes are critical.
3. *Review of Existing Document*: Over the years, most institutions have accumulated a number of somewhat unrelated but significant policies pertaining to personnel. The collation and agreement on these existing policies into a new, more comprehensive and systematic document is essential. Previously recognized benefits must be dealt with fairly and sensitively within the new process.
4. *Legal Assistance*: Competent legal advice must be sought throughout the process, including the process of compilation of existing policies and the development of new, more comprehensive policies. This is particularly important in the areas of affirmative action, contracts, termination, grievance procedures and other related matters.
5. *Format*: It is the uniqueness of an individual system that will dictate format of a policy manual. Obviously, there is no one cor-

rect way. Policies, however, should be clear, well-defined, concise, well-organized, and readable. Grouping related items in consecutive sections is one way. Another would be simply to write policy by policy, perhaps in alphabetical order. A suggestion would be to poll employees and supervisors to determine an acceptable format. One approach would be to provide the finished product to those involved in a loose-leaf binder in order to facilitate periodic manual revision.

6. *Leadership*: Key to keeping the project moving and to bringing it to completion is to name a 10-12 member steering committee or task force. The critical yet time-consuming function of the representative group would be to facilitate and monitor the project to its completion, being cognizant of the key areas of (a) broad participation and (b) the vision of the system as it relates to its personnel. The chairperson of this task force would have the overall responsibility of supervising the task to its effective conclusion.

7. *Style*: Any document relating to personnel should be communicative, personal, and based on a clear understanding and appreciation of what ministry within the church is about.

8. *Revision*: Provisions for annual or biannual revisions or updates should be obvious within the document. Employer and employees must realize that policies are not eternal, but dynamic and based on continual new approaches to good labor-management relations.

PERSONNEL POLICIES OUTLINE

The National Association of Church Personnel Administration has made an excellent contribution to the field of church personnel administration by the publication of *Lay Personnel Policies* by Sister Barbara Garland, S.C.[6] This manual is written to assist in the development of policies which affect lay personnel who join in the services of dioceses, congregations, agencies and institutions and whose primary aim is the furtherance of the gospel message.

For purposes of clarity and with the permission of Sister Barbara, the suggested comprehensive personnel policies outline stated in her text is presented here. The indicated headings are suggested for inclusion in any comprehensive personnel manual.

Section A: Preliminary Materials:
Introductory materials to a comprehensive personnel policies manual should include a letter or words of greeting from the major employer, a clear statement as to whom these policies apply,

statements from church documents emphasizing social justice dictates, and certain general, more global policy statements not distinctly unique to the institution being described.

It is important to note that non-profit organizations which are not recipients of public funds, such as schools or other church-related institutions, may apply for exemptions from certain civil labor organizations. However, Canon 1286 in the Code of Canon Law reads:

Administrators of Goods:

1. in employing workers should also observe with exactness the civil laws which concern labor and social life, according to the principles handed down by the Church;
2. should pay those who work by contract an equitable and decent wage or salary so that they may provide appropriately for their needs and those of their families.[7]

It is obvious that overall just and equitable approaches to the question of personnel policies should permeate any specific, unique approach to personnel matters within a specific system.

Section B: Employment Categories, Procedures for Hiring

The purposes of this section are to:

1. provide employees with a definitive, clear description of how and where they fit within a particular personnel system. This might relate to benefit eligibility, definition of full and part- time employment, concise definition of position/function, definitions of probation, promotion, transfer and removal.
2. provide employees with procedures for hiring, for applying for other jobs within the system, and all other information related to the hiring process.

Section C: Working Conditions, Salary Information

This section would include very specific information related to the daily operation and routines carried out within the system. It might include working hours, dress codes, lunch hours, coffee breaks, overtime, pay periods, payroll deductions, dates of salary increments, compensatory time provisions, etc. From this breakdown it is obvious that Section C is basic to smooth organizational routines, for it so closely impinges upon the work day and the work environment. A work environment characterized by fair play, consistent enforcement of policy and respect for each individual realizes effective, productive and satisfied employers and employees.

Section D: Benefits

This section should deal very carefully and precisely with areas such as vacations, holidays, medical/personal leave, education benefits, and leaves of absence. In addition, total benefit plans, such as health insurance, retirement benefits, worker's compensation and unemployment insurance, should be specified.

It is important to note that in this category it is critical that specifics be carefully spelled out. Maternity leave, for example, should detail length, notice to employer, relationship to basic sick leave, disability insurance, etc. A distinction between personal and sick days is appropriate as is specifying how many such days may accrue from one year to another.

In this category, as well as in Category C, careful adherence to federal and state regulations for the rights of employees must be the norm.

Section E: Job Performance and Review

This important section deals with employee supervision and evaluation and related conditions of job performance which are essential to carrying out the work of the diocese or institution.

Because this section deals with the growth and development of the employee and with the growth of the relationship between the supervisor and the employee, it should be given particularly careful and clear consideration. It should be stated at the outset that every employee has the right to an evaluation which should be constructive and productive.

It is of considerable importance to follow carefully effective performance appraisal and review principles and techniques as outlined in contemporary business management manuals.

It is interesting to note that work is currently being done on coordinating the job description design with the annual evaluation instrument. This technique is particularly effective with ministers within the church for it clearly delineates specific job responsibilities within a organization without losing either the institution's or the individual's charisms. A example of this technique is the *Management by Development* design, developed by Robert North[8] within the teaching profession. Merit pay, teacher career ladders, teacher incentive plans, are all related to performance appraisal. This correlation has advantages in that the evaluation has a distinct impact on differential wage increments.

All facets of job performance and review need thorough investigation.

Section F: Termination Procedures and Grievance Procedures

Resignation, reduction-in-force, reorganization, or unsatisfactory job performance are all reasons for termination.

Termination procedures should be just, fair and impartial. All details related to termination and the appeal process should be clearly defined so that the rights and responsibilities of employee and employer are safeguarded.

It would be understood that dismissal of an employee occurs only for serious reasons and only after sufficient and documented warnings to the employee about the reasons have been given. A grievance might occur when an employee felt unjustly treated and had grounds for complaint.

In both instances, it is imperative that procedures be properly researched, carefully worked out, and objectively administered. In either case, it must be indicated who the binding party would be in such a decision.

Section G: Administration and Review of Personnel Policies

The comprehensive personnel policies manual should state definitely who is responsible for administering, reviewing and revising the policies stated. Employee advisory boards or grievance review boards may also be appropriate.

Finally, as a point of reference, display 7.1, compiled by Garland, contains a checklist of selected dioceses and other church institutions whose manuals contain the aforementioned sections/items:

GENERAL TOPICS CONTAINED IN REPRESENTATIVE MANUALS

ORGANIZATION PROVIDING POLICY MANUAL	TO WHOM POLICIES APPLY (L / A)	FORMAT	LETTER FROM CHIEF EXECUTIVE	DESCRIPTION OF DIOCESE OR ORGANIZATION	AFFIRMATIVE ACTION STATEMENT	EMPLOYMENT CATEGORIES	HIRING PROCEDURES	WORKING CONDITIONS	PAYROLL INFORMATION	BENEFITS - DAYS, INCLUDING LEAVES OF ABSENCE	BENEFITS - PLANS	JOB PERFORMANCE AND REVIEW	EVALUATION FORM INCLUDED	TERMINATION	GRIEVANCE PROCEDURE	REVIEW/ADVISORY GROUP	PARTICIPATION IN MINISTRY NOTED	JOB CLASSIFICATION SYSTEM	SALARY SCALE ADMINISTRATION	OTHER MAJOR INFORMATION FOUND IN MANUAL
ADRIAN DOMINICANS MOTHERHOUSE	L	T	OTHER	●	●	●		●		●	●	●		●	●		●			
BALTIMORE ARCHDIOCESE	A	2 N	●	●	●	●	●	●		●	●	●	●	●		●		'GEN'L	GEN'L	
CINCINNATI ARCHDIOCESE	L	N	●		(PLAN)	●	●		●	●	●	●	●	●		●				AFFIRMATIVE ACTION PLAN INCLUDED
MIAMI CATHOLIC COMMUNITY SERVICES	A	P	●	●	(PLAN) ●	●			●	●	●	●	●	●		●			GEN'L	DISCIPLINARY ACTION STATEMENT
MINNEAPOLIS/ST. PAUL ARCHDIOCESE	L	P			●	●		●		●	●	●	●	VOLUNTARY ONLY				GEN'L	GEN'L	EXTENSIVE SALARY INFORMATION, EVALUATION
NEWARK ARCHDIOCESE	L	P				●			●	●		●	●	VOLUNTARY ONLY				GEN'L	GEN'L	
RICHMOND DIOCESE	A	T	OTHER	●	●	●	●	●	●	●	●	●		●	●		●		SPE-CIFIC	APPLIES TO ALL DIOCESAN SERVICES INC. PARISHES & SCHOOLS *
SEATTLE ARCHDIOCESE	L	N		●		●	●			●	●	●		●	●	●	●		GEN'L	SEPARATE PERFORMANCE & SALARY POLICY DOCUMENTS
SYRACUSE DIOCESE	A	N 2 T	●	●	●	●	●	●	●	●	●	●		●	●	●	●			
SYRACUSE CATHOLIC SCHOOL SYSTEM	A	T			●	●	●	LOCAL NORMS		●		●		●	●	AD HOC	●			
UNITED STATES CATHOLIC CONF.	A	P			●	●	●	●		●		●		●	●	●		SPE-CIFIC		

FORMAT: POLICY (P), TITLELESS FORMAL (T), PAR. NUMBERING (N), 2 MANUALS

TO WHOM POLICIES APPLY: LAY EMPLOYEES (L), PRIESTS, RELIGIOUS, LAY (A)

* GENERAL INFORMATION OR SPECIFIC INFORMATION GIVEN

* RICHMOND ALSO HAS AN EMPLOYEE ASSISTANCE PROGRAM DESCRIBED.

COMPREHENSIVE PERSONNEL POLICIES CHECKLIST

The task of writing a personnel policies manual is a tedious and challenging one. A comprehensive approach is necessary yet demanding. But in the light of the demands of social justice, the task is compelling and essential.

In order to facilitate the process, an extensive checklist was developed by Michael Bechelli, Director of the Office of Religious Education for the Diocese of Richmond, Virginia.[9] Because of its practicality and relevance, it is reproduced in its entirety here.

Section A-Preliminary Materials

_____ 1. Are the policies based on Church documents such as the following:

    _____ a. *Laborum Exercens*

    _____ b. *Gaudiem et Spes*

    _____ c. Labor Day Statement 1981 USCC

    _____ d. 1983 Revised Code of Canon Law

_____ 2. Are both the employees and the employers identified?

_____ 3. What distinctions in particular items of policy are made between and among the employee groups identified?

_____ 4. Are the items stated as policy able to be upheld?

_____ 5. Is it clear that contractual arrangements may occasionally differ from a given policy?

_____ 6. Is a yearly review of the Personnel Policies and a 3 to 5 year revision schedule provided for?

_____ 7. Are all employees and administrators expected to receive a Policy Manuel?

_____ 8. Would any employee be able to reasonably understand the policies?

_____ 9. Is there a strong commitment on the part of the employer to execute the policies?

_____ 10. Were pre-existing policies or privileges rescinded as a result of these policies?

_____ 11. Were any benefits or policies or privileges rescinded as a result of these policies?

_____ 12. If yes to Number 11, was a collegial agreement or compensation provided?

_____ 13. Were representative employees at all levels involved in the process of creating these policies?

_____ 14. Are the policies in agreement or in conflict with other related employer systems of the Diocese?

_____ 15. Are all employees of the Diocese covered by these policies?

_____ 16. Does the introduction state to whom these policies apply?

_____ 17. Does the introduction contain a letter from the Chief Executive Officer such as the Bishop?

_____ 18. Are general policy statements included from a broader base such as Affirmative Action?

_____ 19. Are individuals identified to whom questions about material in the handbook may be referred?

_____ 20. Is a brief but comprehensive description given of the Diocese?

        _____ a. Territory covered?

        _____ b. Statistical data?

        _____ c. Agencies?

        _____ d. Organizational structure?

_____ 21. Do the policies make an Affirmative Action statement or do they apply for exemption from labor regulations?

_____ 22. Do the policies do less than what civil law requires (see the revised Code of Canon Law)?

_____ 23. Is there an Affirmative Action Plan?

_____ 24. Is there an Equal Opportunity statement?

_____ 25. Is the Affirmative Action Plan referred to in a separate handbook?

_____ 26. Are any provisions made regarding hiring of the handicapped?

Section B-Employment Categories and Procedures for Hiring

_____ 27. Are there different classifications of employees?

_____ 28. Are the following terms defined:

        _____ a. Permanent full-time employee?

        _____ b. Permanent part-time employee?

        _____ c. Hourly/temporary employee?

        _____ d. Exempt/non-exempt employee?

_____ 29. Are hiring procedures outlined?

_____ 30. Are hiring procedures within the system outlined?

_____ 31. Are all agencies and departments expected to have the same procedure?

_____ 32. Are new positions advertised internally before they are advertised externally?

_____ 33. Is there an Affirmative Action Plan which is closely tied to the hiring procedures?

_____ 34. Are married couples allowed to work in the same office, parish, or school?

_____ 35. Is there a probationary period for new employees? How long? When do benefits start to accrue?

_____ 36. Are there any procedures for rehiring former employees?

Section C-Working Conditions and Payroll Information

_____ 37. Are employees expected to provide working conditions description for:

    _____ a. Hours to be worked

    _____ b. Summer hours/seasonal hours

    _____ c. Dress codes

    _____ d. Use of telephone

    _____ e. Lunch hour/coffee breaks

    _____ f. Other conditions

_____ 38. Do the policies state payroll information such as:

    _____ a. Times when employees are paid?

    _____ b. Work time allowed to cash a pay check?

    _____ c. Description/itemization of payroll deductions?

    _____ d. Dates for pay increments?

    _____ e. How to change one's pay status?

_____ 39. Was the State Labor Department contacted for copies of laws pertinent to the above?

_____ 40. Were hours worked expanded by the policies or held by these policies?

_____ 41. Were holidays previously granted diminished by these policies?

_____ 42. Is the work week defined? Lunch and break times defined?

_____ 43. When is overtime paid? Are the rates described?

_____ 44. Who approves overtime? Is assignment of overtime on the basis of seniority avoided?

_____ 45. How are employees required to record their "sign-in" and "sign-out"?

_____ 46. How are records maintained of hours worked by "non-exempt" employees?

_____ 47. Are procedures described for notification in the event of snow-clearing? Are those who do come in paid more than those who don't?

_____ 48. How are absences reported?

_____ 49. Are employees restricted regarding outside employment? May exempt employees serve as consultants?

_____ 50. Are employees allowed to accept from clients:

    _____ a. Money?

    _____ b. Gifts?

_____ 51. Are there company parties, celebrations at which employee attendance is required?

_____ 52. What provisions are made for gifts to employees for:

    _____ a. Birthdays?

    _____ b. Weddings?

    _____ c. Service awards/retirement?

_____ 53. How may employees be reimbursed for travel and other business related expenditures?

_____ 54. Are exempt employees entitled to overtime pay?

_____ 55. May employees cash a payroll check during work hours?

Section D-Benefits

_____ 56. Are differences between/among employee groups specified regarding benefits?

_____ 57. Is it stated whether and to what degree the following are accruable from one year to the next?

    _____ a. Holidays

    _____ b. Vacation

    _____ c. Medical

    _____ d. Personal

_____ 58. Is the period defined within which a year's vacation days might be taken?

_____ 59. Is personal leave defined?

_____ 60. Are wages paid during:

    _____ a. Jury duty?

    _____ b. Military duty?

_____ 61. What days (if any) are allowed for death within the family?

_____ 62. Are "family" members defined?

_____ 63. When are leaves of absences permitted?

_____ 64. After a leave of absence, is it clear to which job the employee will return?

_____ 65. What is the maximum length of a leave of absence?

_____ 66. Are benefit plans specified for the following:

    _____ a. Health insurance?

    _____ b. Retirement/pension benefits?

_____ c. Worker's Compensation?

_____ d. Unemployment Compensation?

_____ e. Other, such as disability?

_____ 67. When may a new employee begin to take vacation?

_____ 68. May an employee choose to work instead of taking vacation?

_____ 69. Is there a maximum or minimum number of vacation days which an employee may take at any one time?

_____ 70. Are permanent part-time employees given vacation?

_____ 71. Will accrued vacation pay be given at the time of severance? (check state laws)

_____ 72. Will a person on leave of absence accrue:

      _____ a. Vacation time?

      _____ b. Leave?

      _____ c. Personal time?

_____ 73. Are the employer's needs considered in determining when an employee takes a vacation?

_____ 74. May personal time be accumulated?

_____ 75. Are holidays listed?

_____ 76. Are employer/employees allowed to take religious holidays without pay?

_____ 77. What happens if a holiday occurs during an employee's vacation? What pay is given for work on a holiday?

_____ 78. How long must a new employee wait for coverage by group insurance, or for investiture in the retirement plan?

_____ 79. Are handbooks for group health insurance and retirement available and mentioned in the policies?

_____ 80. Is provision made for a Disability Leave of Absence? How is pregnancy leave related to disability leave?

_____ 81. Is the federal law requiring allowance for military leave of absence (National Guard or Reserve) included?

_____ 82. Is there a statement regarding jury service which reflects local laws?

_____ 83. Are there policies governing attendance at and defining the following? For each category of employee?

      _____ a. Seminars, symposiums

      _____ b. Inservice meetings

      _____ c. Hearings

      _____ d. Classes

_____ 84. To what extent are employees reimbursed for tuition and travel for the above items?

Section E-Job Performance and Review

_____ 85. Is confidentiality addressed regarding employee evaluation?

_____ 86. Are health problems part of the job performance criteria?

_____ 87. Is personal appearance part of the job performance criteria?

_____ 88. When are employee's wages reviewed (anniversary of employment? other times?)?

_____ 89. Are raises based on merit? or on other factors such as cost-of-living?

_____ 90. When/how frequently are employees evaluated?

_____ 91. When are evaluations necessarily written?

_____ 92. Are the two-fold purposes of evaluation emphasized (i.e. growth of individual and improvement of performance)?

_____ 93. Are categories for evaluation addressed?

_____ 94. Are any performance review forms provided?

_____ 95. What role does the job description have in the performance review?

_____ 96. Are there other criteria beyond the job description used for evaluation?

_____ 97. Are issues of chemical dependency, alcoholism and other personally and professionally disruptive patterns of behavior addressed by an Employee Assistance Program?

_____ 98. What connection exists between performance review and merit pay?

_____ 99. May/how will an employee's pay be reduced because of lateness?

Section F-Termination and Grievance Procedures

_____ 100. Are reasons given for termination of employment (i.e., resignation, fiscal constraints, staff reduction or reorganization, unsatisfactory job performance?

_____ 101. How much notice is expected of employee or employer for termination/resignation?

_____ 102. May insurance plans be continued in the case of resignation or termination?

_____ 103. The necessity of at least one formal written warning of unsatisfactory performance before termination included?

_____ 104. Is the principle of subsidiarity evident in the grievance procedure?

_____ 105. Is the grievance procedure separated from the due process procedure?

_____ 106. Are both employee and employer equally represented in the grievance procedure?

_____ 107. How is severance pay determined? by seniority?

_____ 108. Is there provision for an exit interview? and are the exit interview purposes described?

Section G-Administration and Review of Personnel Policies

_____ 109. Who administers the personnel policies?

_____ 110. Who reviews and revises the personnel policies?

_____ 111. Are employees from each of the groups represented on an advisory board or committee?

_____ 112. Where is the employee's personnel record maintained?

_____ 113. How may an employee or others have access to the personnel file?

ADVANTAGES

It is safe to assume that most institutions within the church, particularly Catholic schools, function according to a clearly articulated and cooperatively designed philosophy and mission statement. It is further understood that these standards and guidelines direct the behavior of individuals who work within a particular system. A set of comprehensive personnel policies gives substance, reality and credibility to somewhat lofty ideals.

The advantages of developing and implementing a set of formal personnel policies are many.

1. The administration of personnel policies is a clear example of practicing stated pastoral and ethical values.

2. The careful implementation of well-developed personnel policies facilitates decision-making. Very little guessing ensues. The use of personnel policies avoids the necessity of either an employer or an employee having to make a "new" decision in every situation.

3. Personnel policies, if properly executed, ensure equitable, fair and consistent treatment to all who are employed.

4. Personnel policies eliminate ambiguity and facilitate the management function.

5. Worker's morale and resulting productivity is enhanced by the

communication function inherent in a set of personnel policies.

6. In a set of truly "comprehensive," diocesan-wide personnel policies, one set of rules again emphasizes the one direction of educational ministry within the church. All who minister are treated equitably, whether they are school employees or parish staff. All ministers are valued and "connected" by common bond of faith and service.

PROBLEMS OF PRACTICE

The disadvantage or problems encountered in utilizing a set of comprehensive personnel policies are normally encountered in the implementation phase. They may be, however, the direct result of poor policy development or ineffective policy promulgation.

For example, if the following ineffectiveness factors are allowed to be part of the development phase, the corresponding problems may occur:

Factor	Problem Encountered
1. Insufficient time allotted to develop truly comprehensive policies, cursorily written; gaps and omissions discovered "after the fact."	1. Continued individual and inconsistent interpretation of some critical areas of work.
2. Insufficient discussion allowed during development phase on policy issues conducive to a variety of positions; true consensus not a priority.	2. Certain segment of ministers could be opposed to specific policies and/or to the movement.
3. Lack of clarity in development; of definition between principle, policy and procedure	3. Individual interpretations lack clarity on part of employer and employee. Frustration ensues with countless interpretation questions.
4. Lack of understanding in development and promulgation stage as to exactly who the policies are written for and why policies were developed.	4. The understandable sense that these policies will not affect certain groups, that they pertain only, perhaps, to the religious men and women working in the church. Also if the proper pastoral and ethical dimensions of these policies are not clearly articulated, church workers may view them as oppressive, burdensome, and signifying a lack of trust on the part of church hierarchy.

In the absence of either a personnel office or a personnel director, the successful utilization of comprehensive personnel policies seriously diminishes the chore of successful implementation. The administration of the personnel function, when consistent, fair, and flexible, is the greatest asset to the diminishment of problems potentially encountered. Creative leadership in development and knowledgeable leadership in the implementation stage are key factors.

Problems may also be encountered if the consultation is not allowed to continue through the implementation stage. Additionally, it should be continually reemphasized that the policies are dynamic, flexible and procedurally subject to periodic revision.

Comprehensive personnel policies may be a burden for smaller schools or parish staffs to administer. Assistance in implementation should always be factored in for those groups in need of help.

THE CATHOLIC SCHOOL

This section is written for anyone who is involved in the teaching mission of the church. Clearly the emphasis is on Catholic schools. However, a set of "comprehensive" personnel policies, while touching each facet of school personnel questions, must necessarily speak in a more universal manner. Personnel policies, to be truly comprehensive, should embrace all employer-employee relationships, both religious and lay, within the diocesan church. Personnel policies should not work merely to the benefit of those who minister within the Catholic school.

Acting responsibly as employer and employee and working cooperatively toward a common goal of justice in the area of employment is the challenge presented to everyone who ministers in Christ's name. The Catholic school, as a valued expression of the educational ministry of the church, should be at the forefront of modeling shared responsibility and freedom for all men and women who serve.

SUMMARY

1. The people who consistently and courageously answer the call to serve the educational ministry of the church must be given the opportunity to fully develop as free and respected human beings.
2. Social justice principles and the establishment of the dignity of personhood and work permeate church teachings and papal pronouncements. Employers' and employees' needs are currently in the forefront of "church personnel" dialogue.

3. Comprehensive personnel policies attempt in an orderly fashion to recognize and unify all ministries within the church. They also establish statements which uniformly protect the rights and responsibilities of all who minister within the church.

4. Comprehensive personnel policies are effective only to the degree that (1) consultation, (2) collective and personal ownership (3) legal and technical advice, (4) style and format, (5) leadership at every stage, and (6) flexibility and a sensitive perspective are part of both the development and implementation stages.

5. A comprehensive personnel policies manual should touch every dimension of both the employer-employee relationship and the daily dynamics of the workplace. A good document is clear, concise, thorough and professionally presented to individuals who are affected by it.

6. The advantage in using a set of personnel policies are numerous: (1) social justice ideals are put into practice; (2) decision-making is facilitated; (3) fair and consistent treatment of all employees is the norm; (4) communication and efficient supervision is realized.

7. Problems may be encountered in utilizing comprehensive personnel policies, particularly if the development stage is not properly planned and executed. A personnel office is essential to the efficacious implementation of any personnel policies, particularly if the persons in this office directly responsible for the promulgation of policies have a sense of what it means to minister within the church.

8. To be truly comprehensive, personnel polices must encompass all ministers and ministries within the diocesan church. The Catholic school, because of its prominence and importance in the mission of education, can be an instigator of the movement toward justice and shared responsibility for all.

FOOTNOTES

1. Austin Flannery, O.P., Editor, "The Church in the Modern World" (Gaudium et Spes) in *Vatican Council II, The Conciliar and Post Conciliar Documents* (Collegeville, Minn.: The Liturgical Press, 1975), #25.

2. United States Catholic Conference Office of Domestic Social Development, *1981 Labor Day Statement* (Washington, D.C.: United States Catholic Conference, 1981), p. 2.

3. Synod of Bishops. *Justice in the World* (Washington: United States

Catholic Conference, 1972), p. 44.

4. Pope John Paul II. *Laborem Exercens (On Human Work)*. Printed in *Origins* (NC Documentary Service, September 24, 1981), #6.

5. Rev. Donald G. McCarthy, "The Catholic Vision of Work in the World," in *Issues in the Labor Management Dialogue: Church Perspectives,* Adam Maida, editor (St. Louis: Catholic Health Association of the United States, 1982), pp. 1-11.

6. Sister Barbara Garland. *Lay Personnel Policies* (Cincinnati, Ohio: National Association of Church Personnel Administrators, 1982), pp. 6-24.

7. Canon Law Society of America. *Code of Canon Law: Latin-English Edition* (Washington, D.C.: Canon Law Society of America, 1982), p. 459.

8. Robert W. North. *Management by Development* (Richmond, Va.: Management Explorations, Inc., 1984).

9. Michael Bechelli, "A Checklist for Personnel Policies in Catholic Dioceses and Religious Communities." Paper submitted to Virginia Commonwealth University, Richmond, Virginia, April 25, 1983.

10. Garland, p. 5. It is based on Sister Barbara Garland's *Lay Personnel Policies* previously outlined in this chapter. It is also based on an article, "How to Write a Personnel Manual," by Edgar S. Ellman.

SUGGESTED READINGS

In addition to the references previously identified, the following resources should prove beneficial in this area:

All of the following are from National Association of Church Personnel Administrators Resource Library, 100 E. Eighth Street, Cincinnati, Ohio 45202.

Gehring, Jane. *Personnel Management: A Manual for Parish Leaders.* A hands-on manual for busy parish leaders and administrators which provides tools to assist them in their personnel related responsibilities.

Harrison, Most Rev. Frank J. *The Church as Employer: Renewal in our Working Relationships.* 1984. In this pastoral statement addressed to the Diocese of Syracuse, Bishop Harrison states clearly and unequivocally his commitment to the church's teaching regarding justice for the worker by applying the principles stated in Conciliar and papal teachings to all who are employed and who serve as volunteers in the church of Syracuse.

Kinsella, John. *In Service to Church Ministers: A Brief Introduction to the Ministry of Church Personnel Administration.* Each chapter in this excellent handbook summarizes an important function of church personnel ministry. Chapter IV, Administrative Functions, analyzes both information system development and policy formulation and planning.

Kinsella, John and Garland, Barbara. *Church Personnel Research and Planning.* This practical guide illustrates step by step how planning can be organized and carried out. In workbook format, it details review of current personnel situations, projection of resources, formulation of policy and priority positions, and the development of strategies in the final document.

Other

Dartnell, Inc. *The Dartnell Personnel Director's Handbook.* Chicago: Dartnell Corp., 1971. This book touches the general dimension of personnel administration. It is a practical approach to the functions specific to management: policy, benefits, services, etc.

Bureau of Law and Business, Inc. *The Personnel Manager's Encyclopedia of Personnel Policies.* Stamford, Conn.: BLB, Inc., 1984. A complete "how-to" preparation handbook to write or revise a personnel policy manual. This manual is not written from a church perspective.

Dartnell, Inc. *How to Develop a Personnel Policy Manual.* Chicago: Dartnell, 1977, 1983. This revised publication is intended as a working tool for management to select those personnel practices and policies best suited to their company and tells how to plan, prepare and produce an actual policy manual. This manual is not written from a church perspective.

Meltzer, H. and Nord, W. R. *Making Organizations Humane and Productive: A Handbook for Practitioners.* New York: Wiley, 1981. This book presents organizational behavior knowledge for use by those who deal administratively with people. It is a collection of essays touching a variety of issues pertinent to personnel policy development.

Katz, Alan S. *The Professional Personnel Policies Guidebook.* Reading, Mass.: Addison-Wesley, 1983. A practical, hands-on document that will assist the practitioner in the development and implementation of personnel policies. This text is not written from a church perspective.